GEORGE HARRISON

LIVING IN THE MATERIAL WORLD

OLIVIA HARRISON

GEORGE HARRISON
LIVING IN THE MATERIAL WORLD

FOREWORD BY MARTIN SCORSESE

INTRODUCTION BY PAUL THEROUX

EDITED BY MARK HOLBORN

ABRAMS, NEW YORK

I have a vivid memory of the first time I heard *All Things Must Pass* when it came out on vinyl in 1970. The packaging was very special, with that haunting, timeless photo of George on the cover, sitting in Friar Park. It was a three-record set, an abundance of new music. And when I dropped the first record over the spindle and put the needle on the first cut, 'I'd Have You Anytime', I was immediately entranced. Something beautiful happened whenever George played the guitar – I'm thinking of that lyrical break on 'You're Gonna Lose That Girl', among so many other magical moments with The Beatles – and here he was revelling in a newfound freedom, making music that was all his own. There was real joy in the sheer act of creativity. And there was a powerful sense of the ritualistic on this album, in the sound he found with Phil Spector. I remember feeling that it had the grandeur of liturgical music, of the bells used in Tibetan Buddhist ceremonies. The wonder I felt the first time I heard that music has never left me.

And that was just the beginning. The cultivation of harmony, balance, serenity – it's there in all of George's music as it was in his life, which were one and the same, I suppose. When we made our movie, I saw that he was always testing himself, pushing past doubt and coming out the other side. The closer I looked at his life and his career, the more I was drawn to him, and to the way he coped with and learned from the peaks and the valleys, those moments when you experience the other side of acclaim and everything comes crashing down around you. It's all very fragile, and he came to understand that, and, ultimately, to see beyond it.

I've always loved George Harrison's music. Through the process of making our picture, I came to love and respect him as a human being.

MARTIN SCORSESE

Introduction

PAUL THEROUX

It is a happy thought that the sweetest music arises from an untroubled heart. The soaring melodies soothe us and make us self-consciously reflect that we're weak and strange and pitiable in our sadness for needing the uplifting syncopation of this encouragement, the reassurance of comforting lyrics. As though from the sky, here is this strong and contented virtuoso – George Harrison, say – whom we envy for being strong, someone supremely contented. What a lucky man to be able to create such harmony and to penetrate our soul; to make us feel better, to help heal us and ease our minds. Isn't it pretty to think so?

The truth is usually the opposite of this. The art that is indestructible and always fresh never comes easy. Its source is typically uncertain or bleak, sometimes harrowing, the pure notes quavering over an abyss of shadows between life and death, that mournful place from which the most passionate yearnings take shape in the form of a song, a poem, a story, a harmonious vision. But even as I write this, speaking of the complex process of creation, words and music made of doubt and the divided self, the conflicts that help us to be sane, and the paradox of opposites, I seem to hear someone mutter over my shoulder, 'Rock music is about as metaphysical as my Aunt Fanny…'

And yet it seems to me impossible to overestimate the resonant clarity of George Harrison's music – his songs of innocence and experience; or the subtle wisdom of his lyrics. Even as a relative youngster, more than thirty years before his untimely death, in his *All Things Must Pass* album, he was singing powerfully of transformation, in the title track, and in 'Art of Dying' and 'Beware of Darkness' and 'What Is Life'. He could be as jolly as his ukulele-strumming hero and namesake, George Formby, but as soon as he seizes our attention with his humour and his teasing, he is reminding us – and himself – that we are mortal and all things end; that the laughter dies, and as one of his fellow English poets put it, 'The woods decay and fall… man comes and tills the field and lies beneath, and after many a summer dies the swan.'

George at his best was a man dedicated to whittling down his ego; he was not one being but many, and he remains an enduring figure of fascination to those of us for whom his music runs through our head, reminding us of better times. It is no wonder he was so passionate: he was himself his own wicked twin. Although he was deliberately elusive, self-deprecating, hard to pin down, the inescapable description that one can apply to him is that he was also his opposite. He made no bones about this and, a hater of pomposity in all forms, he expressed it with characteristic downrightness:

'I have this kind of strange thing,' he said, 'and I put it down to being a Pisces. Pisces is the sign of two fish. The way I see it is that one half is going where the other half has just been. I was in the West and I was into rock 'n' roll, getting crazy, staying up all night and doing whatever was supposed to be the wrong things. That's in conflict with all the right things, which is what I learned through India – like getting up early, going to bed early, taking care of yourself and having some sort of spiritual quality to your life. I've always had this conflict.'

He was at odds with himself, but who isn't? In that respect – 'living proof of all life's contradictions,' as he put it – he resembles most of us. We recognise him as a kindred soul in his contradictions – and though his life was lived on a vast scale, he was unusually truthful, and in his songs much more explicit than we dare to be. He made it his mission to explore his contradictions in his own way, through his music. So, to say that he was one of the great musicians of his time – one of the most innovative guitarists ever, one of the most imaginative songwriters – is to give only part of the story. 'The quiet one' is the stereotypical description of the man – but he was on fire within. He was himself the dark and the light, the flames and the ashes. To make music that mattered over the years, to bring renewal with each work, he seemed determined to burn out one self after another.

'He had karma to work out,' his widow, Olivia, is on the record as saying, 'and he wasn't going to come back and be bad. He was going to be good and bad and loving and angry and everything all at once. You know, if someone said to you, "Okay, you can go through your life and you can have everything in five lifetimes, or you can have a really intense one and have it in one, and then you can go and be liberated," he would have said, "Give me the one, I'm not coming back here."'

I also think there's a stark difference between 'contradiction' and 'confusion'. He wasn't confused; had he been he would have found it impossible to search and learn with such clear-sightedness. His friend and mentor Ravi Shankar said that George exhibited *tyagi*, a Sanskrit term for a feeling of nonattachment or renunciation. Ravi wondered how this aspect of enlightenment could have come so clearly to a worldly lad from Liverpool. It doesn't seem odd to me that this thoughtful man came to feel the sense of freedom bordering on exultation that mendicants experience in nonattachment. But it is a notable, and noble, quality in a rock star to practise it, as George did.

We all feel that we could do a bit better in our lives; in the secret history of this imaginative soul, George was active in pursuing this path. Surely it arose in large part from his having had everything while still young. At the age of nineteen or twenty he was on top of the world in every sense – inspiring the world to sing and dance. Performing with The Beatles gave him joy – gave us all joy. But he did not see this exuberance as a final fulfilment; the very fact of The Beatles as a musical and financial phenomenon made him doubtful enough to begin to look for a higher meaning, and, after The Beatles, to go on looking. He knew that he was living in the material world, but had he been so attached to it he would not have been able to look deeper into it.

Early in his life as a musician, towards the end of the explosive new sound of The Beatles (and explosive in much more than music, it was a seismic shift in popular culture), George found his way to India. Through music and meditation, and the mantras that he chanted until the very end of his life, he was drawn to an unselfish, and ultimately a more mystical, view of the world. The man who could make a whole stadium rock began to see silence as another ideal. He has described himself as an idle, smirking, doodling student at school, and yet in India he became devout and studious, a reader of the swamis – notably, Swami Vivekananda. He negotiated this path with Ravi as a friend and mentor, but without any sanctimony, celebrating the natural order of things, finding peace in the Eastern system of belief. In this pantheon of luminous, often multi-armed and gesticulating gods, nothing is simple.

Hinduism is not a religion of spotless saints or martyred virgins. There is hardly a Hindu god that is not many-dimensional, a disparate combination of contrasting features. The Hindu gods – and there are said to be millions of them – are heroic; they fly, they fight, some are part animal, like the elephantine Ganapati, or the monkey god Hanuman. The god of love, Kamadeva, uses his bow fashioned of sugarcane (and his bow-string of honeybees) to shoot arrows made of flowers. Many are musical – Saraswati, who is usually depicted plucking the sitar-like stringed *veena*; Krishna, the blue god (for whom George had a distinct affinity), plays a flute. In Hindu belief there is no such thing as undiluted brightness, but always the cycle of darkness and light, mingled creation and destruction, the one necessary to the other. Discovering this view of the world was a liberation for George, and an inspiration to him as a musician. In India he was given heart and a direction. 'None of us can relate to each other unless we can relate to ourselves,' he said at a UNICEF press conference in 1974; 'we must find ourselves really.'

The greatest trauma of his life was his waking to the sound of his house – this safe place – being broken into, at four-thirty in the morning. 'Somebody's smashed a window,' Olivia said. And George faced a horror that few of us will ever know: a demented stranger urgent to murder him in the dark. The woman George had fallen in love with for her beauty and humour and vitality – a woman slight of build, an adoring and comforting presence in his life, was transformed by the intrusion that night from a sprite into a warrior-goddess.

George was the traveller who, against the odds, came back from the dead. And the murder attempt seems to have destroyed the darker part of him, and left him pondering.

'I was lying there. I can't believe it,' he said to Olivia. 'After all I've been through – I'm being murdered in my own house. And because of that I'd better start letting go of this life so that I can do what I've been practising to do my whole life.'

What has become apparent in the decade since his death is the uncanny symmetry of George's life – a life lived to the fullest. What might have seemed random or impulsive in him while he lived, is in retrospect a pattern; part performance, part pilgrimage. His saturation in the material world drove him to seek the spiritual in things – and so his life seems a series of vanishings and reappearances, journeys there and back, even the portraits of him that seem iconic are various, a progression of so many faces, his features, his hair, his posture – different in each one. Yet his gaze is unchanged, his eyes telling us that the same soul is inhabiting this body.

All this sounds solemn, but he was a man of subtle and often self-mocking humour. George was interested in many things beside music, and although music was his first love, he was vitalised by travel, movie making, car racing. Look at his friends – the Pythons Gilliam and Idle, and Jackie Stewart, Billy Preston, Eric Clapton, Bob Dylan: the funniest men on the planet, the fastest, his most brilliant contemporaries in music.

But equal to his passion for music, and his diverse and close friendships, was an overwhelming desire to get back to earth – literally so – to dig, to plant trees, to surround himself with flowers that he himself had grown. The most obvious characteristic of the houses that he built, or bought and fixed up in the course of his life, are the gardens he planned and planted. No matter how extraordinary the houses, the gardens he created around them surpassed the bricks and mortar.

A gardener is inevitably someone with humility, who sees that these trees will eventually tower over and outlive him; the gardener is generous, optimistic, nurturing, taking pleasure in the planting but also making something beautiful for others. In George's case the gardens he made gave him the sense that he was living in isolation, on an island of his own making: '…it's great when I'm in my garden, but the minute I go out the gate I think: "What the hell am I doing here?"'

'From the day I met him he was defiant,' Olivia said, 'and so determined that nothing was going to stop him from leaping as far as he could.'

She was thinking of his words in the song 'Run of the Mill':

How high will you leap?
Will you make enough for you to reap it?
Only you'll arrive – at your own made end
With no one but yourself to be offended –
It's you that decides.

1

After the Bombs

There was an honesty that we had, a very simple, naïve honesty, and I think that had a lot to do with where we came from. The people up there have a certain naïve honesty and humour. They say you have to have humour to live in a place like that. Everybody who comes out of Liverpool thinks they are comedians, and we were no exception. That kept us going.   GEORGE

Liverpool Cathedral and bomb-damaged buildings, 1942

18   Damaged power lines after a bombing raid, Liverpool, 1941

During the war, Liverpool was the second biggest port in the empire, after London, with huge docks. It really did get hammered in the Blitz. You hear the story about Aunt Mimi dodging the bombs, going to the hospital when John was born. That's not an exaggeration. Liverpool got the shit bombed out of it.

Post-war, our playgrounds were bombsites, which could be pretty dangerous. You got streets that just went off into nothing. We were very aware of the war. Near where George, Paul and I went to school at the Liverpool Institute, there was a church called St Luke's that had been firebombed. The whole church was just a burned-out shell. It's still there now as a reminder.

There would always be a few kids who didn't have a father. It was never talked about, but you didn't know whether they were children of an American soldier or whether their father had died in the war. NEIL ASPINALL, *Lifelong friend, CEO Apple Corps*

22   George, aged two, being held by his sister, Louise, with brothers Peter and Harry (far right of table), Liverpool, V.E. Day, 1945

I had two brothers and one sister. My sister was twelve when I was born. My father was driving a bus at the time. He used to be a seaman. I lived in a two-up-two-down, 12 Arnold Grove, which in those days didn't have bathrooms or jacuzzis or things like that, it just had a little zinc bathtub which would be hanging on the backyard wall. My mother was from an Irish family called French, and she had lots of brothers and sisters. My grandmother used to live in Albert Grove, which was next to Arnold Grove, so when I was small I could go out the back door and around the back entries – which they used to call jiggers in Liverpool – go around the back jigger and into my grandmother's house. So they were my earliest recollections. GEORGE

Left, Harry, George, brother Harry, Peter and sister Louise, North Wales, 1947
Above, Louise and Harry Harrison, George's mother and father, at a dance, late 1940s 25

Peter, Louise, George and Harry, late 1940s
Right, George, late 1940s

Pages 28–29, Dovedale School Admissions Registry Book 1943–1955, showing George's registration on 19 April 1948

LIVERPOOL EDUCATION COMMITTEE.

.... School

.... Department

ADMISSION AND WITHDRAWAL REGISTER

From 19 1943

To 19 1955

DAVIS & MOUGHTON, LTD., EDUCATIONAL PUBLISHERS, BIRMINGHAM.

Admission Number	Date of Admission			Date of Re-admission			CHILD'S NAME IN FULL (Surname first).	Date of Birth.			ADDRESS	Whether exempt from Religious Instruction
	Day	Mth	Year	Day	Mth	Year		Day	Mth	Year		
851	19	4	48				Heston Janice	19	4	43	20 Stalbridge Avenue	No
852	19	4	48				Peart David Alex	16	3	43	22 A. Allerton Road	" "
853	19	4	48				Falconer Denis	27	4	42	9 Zetland Road	"
854	19	4	48				Taylor Michael George	3	3	43	27 Karslake Road	"
855	19	4	48				Cotton Alan	12	3	43	25 Elmbank Road	"
856	19	4	48				Thomas David	12	4	43	102 Herondale Rd	"
857	19	4	48				Filson David Alex	16	4	43	Flat 2. 24 Arundel Ave.	"
858	19	4	48				Walker Colin	19	4	43	50 Earlsfield Rd	"
859	19	4	48				Pomford Douglas C	27	4	43	68 Fallowfield Rd	"
860	19	4	48				Gidman Peter John	2	5	43	14 Ashdale Rd	"
861	19	4	48				Tye Barry Delmar.	3	5	43	6 Gorsedale Rd	"
862	19	4	48				Davenport Anthony J.	22	5	43	104 Barndale Rd	Yes
863	19	4	48				Scragg David A.	25	5	43	8 Belhaven Rd	No
864	19	4	48				Coalsting Norman A	28	5	43	140 Pittville Avenue	No
865	19	4	48				Andrews John R.	1	6	43	25 Barndale Rd	"
866	19	4	48				Gurrow Sheila J.	26	1	43	28 Prince Alfred Rd	"
867	19	4	48				Drabble Dorothy E.	22	2	43	15 Hallville Rd	"
868	19	4	48				Romney Valerie	12	3	43	16 Ivydale Rd	"
869	19	4	48				Cheevers Barbara	13	3	43	20 Gresford Ave.	"
870	19	4	48				Winstanley Margaret A	15	3	43	187 Rose Lane	"
871	19	4	48				McCartew Ann	19	3	43	77 Crawford Avenue	"
872	19	4	48				Mills Jacqueline	26	3	43	91 Garmoyle Rd	"
873	19	4	48				Williams Patricia Y.	4	4	43	4 Hartdale	"
874	19	4	48				Burke Helen Marg.	1	5	43	20 Oakdale Rd	"
875	19	4	48				Apter Ruth	7	5	43	69 Russell Rd	"
876	19	4	48				Hatkinson Eunice B	10	5	43	4 Elmbank Rd	"
877	19	4	48				Robinson Pauline	20	5	43	32 Cranford Ave.	"
878	19	4	48				Lomax Barbara	1	6	43	69 Alverstone Rd	"
879	19	4	48				Harrison George	25	2	43	12 Arnold Grove	yes
880	26	4	48				Wright Robert Charles	5	8	40	42 Pittville Road	No
881	26	4	48				Power Kenneth John	16	2	43	57 Croxteth Road	"
882	28	4	48				Williams Peter	21	8	43	10 Stanley Terrace	"
883	28	4	48				Williams Michael	21	8	43	10 Stanley Terrace	"
884	3	5	48				Young Alan John	16	3	43	5 Boxdale Road	"
885	3	5	48				(Butt) Flanbury Margaret	6	4	43	225 Rose Lane	"
886	3	5	48				Burkey Diane	25	5	43	67 Boxdale Rd	"
887	3	5	48				Edge Lawrence	8	5	43	11 Belhaven Rd	"
888	10	5	48				Robertson Freda M.	29	6	43	5 Bromley Avenue	"
889	10	5	48				Dobbs Jasmine H.M.	27	3	43	20 Harthill Ave.	"
890	10	5	48				Owen Doreen	15	7	43	2 Duddingston Ave	"

Margin notes: "now spruce adopted" (beside 861); "991" (beside 884); "✓" marks beside 878 and 886.

George came to Dovedale Road at the same time John Lennon was there, alongside other names like Jimmy Tarbuck. Dovedale Road was a junior school. There you did what used to be called the eleven-plus exam to see if you were smart enough to get into a grammar school, or if you went up to a secondary modern, and George passed his eleven-plus and went to the Liverpool Institute.

I always remember my Mum saying that they had been on the housing list to have another house for twenty-two years. In 1949 they eventually did get a house, and we moved to Speke in about 1950. Speke was a building site basically; there were no roads or anything. It was like two feet of mud everywhere. But it was a bigger house. PETER HARRISON, *Brother*

George at Dovedale Infants/Junior School, Liverpool (George is in the back row, fifth from right), 1950s

Right, Cover of *Dark Horse* album by George showing teachers and pupils from the Liverpool Institute High School

There were numerous parks around Liverpool. People always think that Liverpool's a big built-up city, but if you could see it from the air I think you'd realise there are more parks there than in the majority of cities. When you were a little one you played on the bombsites but by and large weekends as a family we always used to go to a park somewhere – take some sandwiches and a bottle of water. HARRY HARRISON, *Brother*

I used to live in a place called Speke, which is on the outskirts of Liverpool. My mother was a midwife, so she would keep getting moved to the outskirts. The roads were kind of unmade when we got there. It was frontier land. And George lived just down the road. It was a bus stop away. It was a road called Central Avenue, which was the main road, and then there was Western Avenue, and then half an hour away was the city, where our school was. And we both went to the same school. I would get on the bus, and then a stop later George would get on. So I'd see this kid with a quiff, but younger than me, so I wouldn't pay much attention, because I was cooler, I was older. But eventually he must have had a seat next to me on the bus, so that's how we met. Obviously going to the same school we had a bond. And then it turned out that we both loved rock 'n' roll, and guitars. He was a cocky little guy. He had a good sense of himself; he wasn't cowed by anything. He had a great haircut.

Looking back now, it was pre-fame – we were just ordinary kids who couldn't get in places because we weren't famous. Teachers didn't like us. Rock 'n' roll hadn't properly arrived yet. I always think of it as kind of Dickensian. And the school that I went to with George, incidentally, was a very Dickensian old place. In fact, Dickens had talked there. That's how Dickensian it was. You grew up wanting to go somewhere else. It made you hungry, so art was a great golden vision. For us, we wouldn't have called it art, but rock 'n' roll. PAUL McCARTNEY

When I was about twelve or thirteen there was a guy who used to go to the junior school I went to who had this guitar he was selling. It cost me three pounds ten shillings – about ten dollars. Just a little cheap acoustic guitar. But I didn't really know what to do with it. I noticed that where the neck fitted on the box it had a big bolt through it holding it on, and I thought, oh, that's interesting. I unscrewed it and the neck fell off. And I was so embarrassed that I couldn't get it back together I hid it in the cupboard for a while. Later my brother fixed it.   GEORGE

I fixed one that had literally bent in the middle. There was a strap inside that was shorter than the guitar, so when I screwed it up it pulled it straight. We used that on stage, because we had a skiffle group going. We used to do the working men's clubs, like the British Legion and all that, for five bob a night and all you could drink.   PETER HARRISON

We were trying to think of a name and I had just seen *Rebel Without a Cause*, so I said, 'What about the Rebels?' So, we called ourselves the Rebels. We got Peter, George's older brother, to teach us bass and we went to the local British Legion Club, which was an ex-servicemen's club. I think there were about six people in there standing at the bar drinking, but it was a gig for us. When we got to the end of our repertoire, we just sang them all again. By the time we got back we were really excited. Poor old Pete's fingers were bleeding because he'd been thumping away at this piece of string for the last hour and a half. That was really the start of it. But that was our one and only gig.

My sister married an American merchant seaman called Red. He used to make periodic trips from New York to Liverpool and one particular day he came in with some records. There's this EP – I think it was pink and pale-green – of this guy with his mouth open playing his guitar. I looked at the name and I had to laugh: he isn't called Elvis! But I put it on, and that was it: 'Wow!' Immediately I had to tell George about this. 'Have you heard this guy Elvis Presley? He's phenomenal!' Consequently, skiffle went out the door and it was rock 'n' roll.

Also among the records was 'That'll Be the Day' by Buddy Holly and the Crickets. It hadn't even aired in England by this time. I put it on, and again this was something completely new. So I took it up to George and said, 'Listen to this, George,' and he said, 'Oh, that's really good. Can I borrow it?' So I loaned him this little 45. A week later, I go up to see him and he's learned the intro, all the chords, the guitar break – the lot. This is what amazed me about George: he had this ability to memorise things.   ARTHUR KELLY, *School friend*

George on the beach with his brother Peter, father Harry and family friends, 1950s

Page from George's school exercise book, 1950s
Right, George on a racing motorcycle, Aintree Racecourse, Liverpool, 1950s

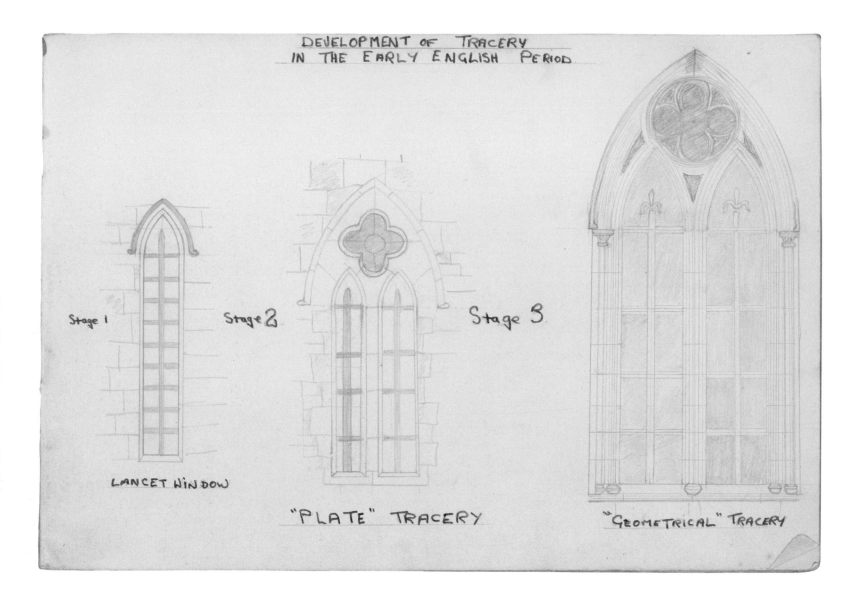

DEVELOPMENT OF TRACERY
IN THE EARLY ENGLISH PERIOD

Stage 1

Stage 2

Stage 3

LANCET WINDOW

"PLATE" TRACERY

"GEOMETRICAL" TRACERY

Me and George. Oh man, I had the best times with George. We hitch-hiked to a place in Wales called Harlech when we were kids, before The Beatles, and we just hitch-hiked our way there. We'd heard a song, 'Men of Harlech', and saw a signpost – 'Yeah!' There was a big castle, and we just went. We had our guitars, took them everywhere, and ended up in this café. We tried to go to a central meeting place in Harlech, and it was this little café. It had a jukebox, so it was home, and we sat around there. We met a guy and started talking. He was into rock 'n' roll and so we went and stayed at his house. It was great. Me and George top-and-tailing in a bed. And he had a mother! It was kind of a bed and breakfast, but we didn't realise. Years later we realised we hadn't paid anyone, and now we were rich and famous. She wrote to us and we said 'Oh, sorry! Herewith payment.' But it was great, we just had so many laughs. Just with these guys, these Welsh guys. One was called John and the other was Aniron – a big Welsh guy who played bass. We sat in with their band one drunken night in a Welsh pub. PAUL McCARTNEY

Postcard from George and Paul to George's mother, Louise, from Exmouth during their hitch-hiking trip, August, 1959

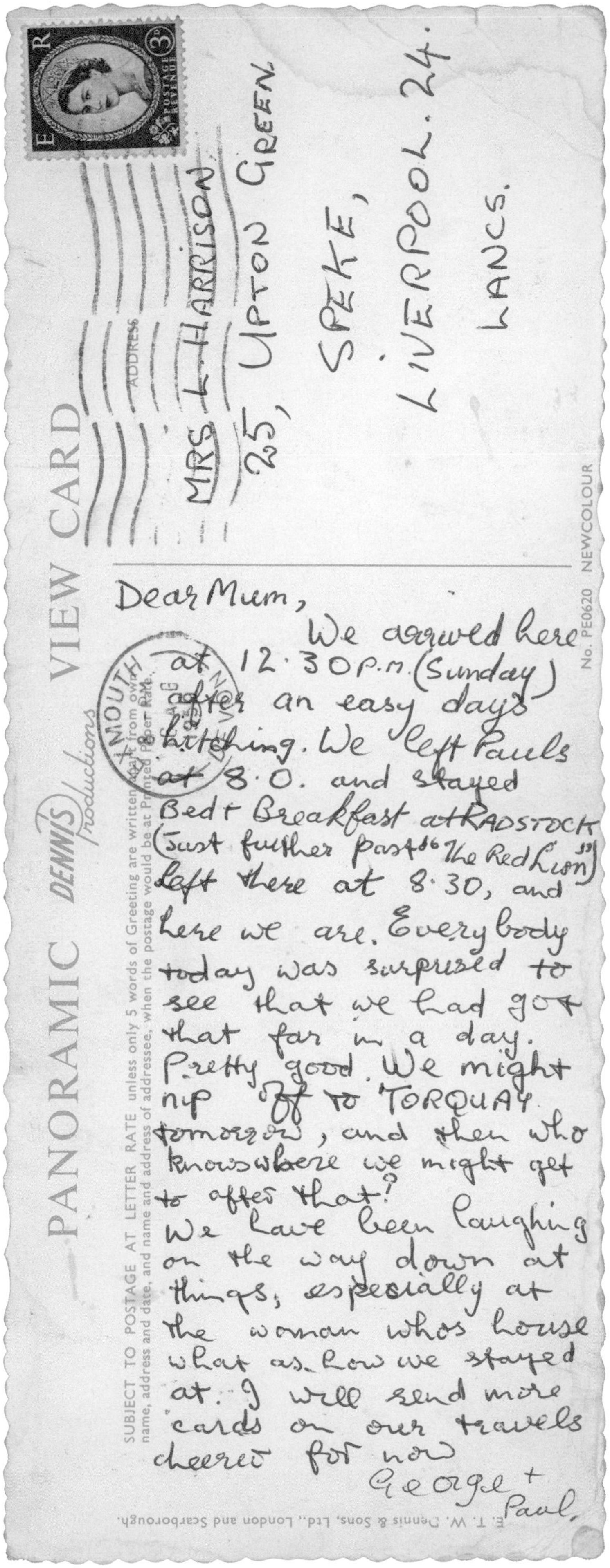

PANORAMIC VIEW CARD

DENNIS Productions

SUBJECT TO POSTAGE AT LETTER RATE unless only 5 words of Greeting are written apart from own name, address and date, and name and address of addressee, when the postage would be at Printed Paper Rate.

ADDRESS

MRS L. HARRISON,
25, UPTON GREEN,
SPEKE,
LIVERPOOL. 24.
LANCS.

No. PE0620 NEWCOLOUR

Dear Mum,
We arrived here at 12.30 p.m. (Sunday) after an easy days hitching. We left Pauls at 8.0. and stayed Bed + Breakfast at RADSTOCK (Just further past "The Red Lion") Left there at 8.30, and here we are. Everybody today was surprised to see that we had got that far in a day. Pretty good. We might nip off to TORQUAY tomorrow, and then who knows where we might get to after that?
We have been laughing on the way down at things, especially at the woman whos house what as how we stayed at. I will send more cards on our travels
cheerio for now
George + Paul.

E. T. W. Dennis & Sons, Ltd., London and Scarborough.

We needed a good guitar player. Both John and I played a bit, but we couldn't really solo. We weren't that good. And I said, 'I know this guy. He's a bit young, but he's good.' John said, 'Well, let's meet him, come on.' So I said to George, 'You want to go meet these guys I'm in a group with?' He said, 'Yeah.' So he brought his guitar and we were on the top deck of a double-decker bus in Liverpool around where John lived, a place called Woolton. And nobody was on the bus, late at night, and John said to George, 'Well, go on, let's hear you play.' So I said, 'Go on, get your guitar out.' So George unpacked his guitar, got it out, and he played this thing called, 'Raunchy'. And John and I were like, 'Wow, this guy can play!' That was it. He was in the group. PAUL McCARTNEY

My first guitar was this little cheap thing. Then I got a cello-style F-hole single cutaway – it was a Höfner, which was like the German version of the Gibson. I got a pickup and stuck it on. Then I swapped it for this guitar called a Club 40, which is a little Höfner that looked like a solid guitar but it was actually hollow inside, no sound holes. Then this guitar came along, still made by Höfner, called a Futurama, and it was a dog to play. The worst action. They tried to copy a Fender Strat. It had a great sound, though. It had a real good way of switching in the three pickups and all the combinations.

When we started making a bit of money I saved up seventy-five pounds and I saw an ad in a paper in Liverpool, and there was a guy going to sell this guitar he'd brought back from America, and I went and bought it. It was a Gretsch, the Duo Jet, which is on my *Cloud Nine* album cover. It was my first real American guitar. I tell you, it was second-hand but I polished that thing, and I was so proud to own that. GEORGE

In Upton Green he used to practise a couple of times a week with the whole gang in his bedroom and it used to drive you mad with his stamping foot. All you could hear downstairs was this thump-thump-thump of his foot and Mum and Dad used to go bananas – but they put up with it. PETER HARRISON

His parents were very welcoming to me, when I'd go around the house. His dad was Harry Harrison, who was a bus driver, and a very laconic sort of Liverpool guy – didn't talk that much, very practical. And Louise, his mum, was a blonde lady, Catholic, and tough. I think he got his toughness from her. Once there was somebody who had been knocking at the door, probably junk mail or something, and she got annoyed with him so she went to the upstairs bedroom, poured a tub of water over the guy: 'Go away!' Didn't suffer fools gladly – and neither did George.

George didn't sing too much at the beginning. He was mainly the practical one, the guitar player. I'd sing, or later John would sing. I think I mainly did the singing. George's job when he left school was as an electrician, so he was practical. His dad was a bus driver, his brother worked on the buses, and his family was a very practical family. George loved cars and motorbikes and car racing. He became a great fan of Formula One later. It was always that way. PAUL McCARTNEY

Dean Mrs HORMINSOON

ARE IS VERIG HANSUME TO BEEN
IN HOMBURG AND HAUING SOME GREAT DAY.
I HOP YOU ARE VERIN HOPPING IN ENGLANDS
AND ARE SOOM TOW GOW TOOE CANIDAH TO CANIDAH.
HOO ARE MR HARMIGALOS EH? HIM BUS VERY
GOOD STILL YET? IO HOP PEATRR IS STILL
SELLING HIM MOTA RIKES AND THINGS AND
EVERY ONE A WINNER.

WE'VE MOIT STAG YET
ANOTHER MOONS IN HITLAR AND HAVE MANY MONEYS
AND WE MOIT SPEND HIM TOOO. ARE YOU HAPPPY
WITH KNOWS SONSIN? YOUR HOUSES? ARE YOU?
I THINIC YOU WILL LIKE GORGES WHEN HE COOMB
HOWMB TOW ONGLOOND RECORSPE HEEM
HAB ANEW SHIRT ANEW SHIRT.

OI WOLL CLOSE NOW AS
OI AM FINISHING NOW SOW OI WOLL ENDE IT
ALL. HAPPY KRISHT MOUSES!
            LOUVE JOHN
                 XXXY

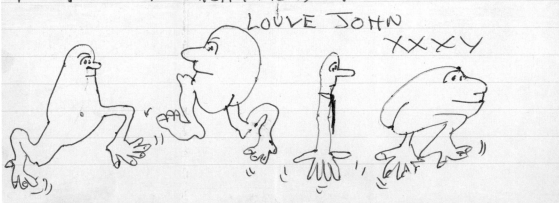

Letter from John to George's mother, Louise, 1960s
Right, George and his mother Louise at home, Upton Green, Speke, Liverpool, 1961

My mother was a real big fan of music and she was really happy about having the guys around. And John was always keen to get out of his house because his Aunt Mimi was kind of very stern and strict. I remember going to John's house once when I first had met him. I was still at the Institute. We were trying to look like Teddy boys, which was the style in those days. And I must have looked pretty good because she didn't like me at all. GEORGE

I was always bad in school. I didn't like it, and I'd always just sit at the back. I've still got some of my books from when I was about thirteen, and there's drawings of guitars and different scratch plates. Always trying to draw Fender Stratocasters.   GEORGE

In the area I come from, in every other house there was a guy in the Merchant Navy, which is where I wanted to go. And they would bring in all the music in from America. We were blessed: it was a port, so guys from New York or New Orleans would bring all this stuff. RINGO STARR

The Canadian Pacific liner *Empress* just before her first post-war voyage to Canada, Liverpool
Right, Lock gates leading from Bramley-Moore Dock into Sanden Half-Tide Dock, Liverpool

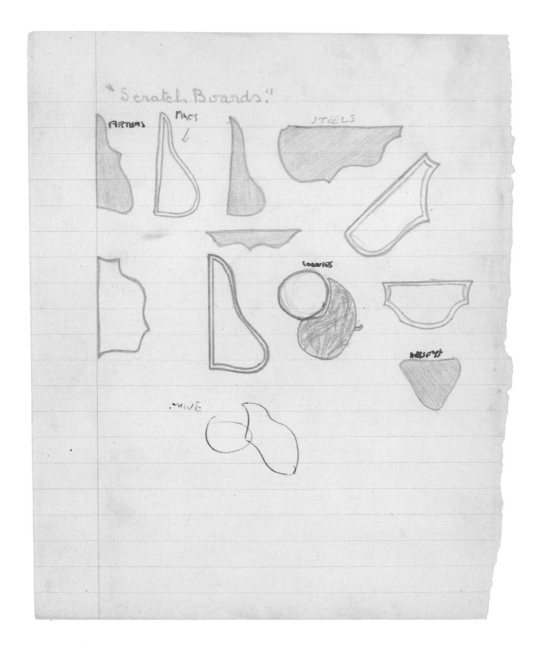

I used to book seats for the theatre because George wanted to see all the acts that were on. He thought Lonnie Donegan was just absolutely wonderful. And I remember taking him to see Joe Brown, that was another one. And he coaxed money out of me to go to the cinema. His love of film was very strong. He used to sneak off school, and sadly I used to give him the money to do it – 'Don't tell your Mum.' IRENE HARRISON, *Sister-in-Law*

Pages from George's school exercise book, 1950s, showing guitar scratch board designs used by various people: Arthur Kelly, Paul McCartney, Tommy Steele, Lonnie Donegan and George himself

O

Lonnie Donegan.

78 revs: Rock Island Line — John Henry.
Lost John — Stewball.
Diggin' my Potatoes — Bury my Body.
Bring a little Water Sylvia — Dead or Alive.
Dont You Rock me Daddy-o. — Alabamy Bound.
Cumberland Gap. — Love is Strange! GAMBLINSMAN PUTING ON THE AGONY

45 revs. E.P. Rock Island Line — John Henry { Lost John — Stewball
Diggin' my Potatoes — Bury my Body } Bring a little water Sylvia
                                                Dead or Alive.
                    _____

Railroad Bill — Stakalee   }
Ballad of Jessee James — Wreck of old 97 }
                    _____

Midnight Special — When the Sun Goes Down }
New Burial Ground — Wrong Man Blues.   }
                    _____

33 revs L.P. The Lonnie Donegan Showcase.
Alabamy Bound, I shall not be moved, Nobody's
Child. How Long, Long Blues, Wreck of the old 97,
Wabash Cannonball. Rambling Man, Frankie and Johnie

INVERNESS CATHEDRAL.

We heard that Larry Parnes was coming up to Liverpool with Billy Fury and they were auditioning back-up bands for Billy Fury – that was the story we got. They were going to use this guy Allan Williams's club. We did actually get a gig from that but it seemed a bit of a shambles. Larry Parnes didn't stand up saying, 'Great, lads!' or anything like that, but we did get the call to go out with Johnnie Gentle and we all schlepped around in a van around the Inverness area, right up north of Scotland. We thought we'd better get some great stage names too. Stuart was into some painter so he was called Stuart De Staël, Paul was Paul Ramon, and I was Carl Harrison. Funny really, doesn't sound like a stage name now, it's just that I loved Carl Perkins. And John, I think Paul says he was Long John. It was a pretty pathetic tour. By the end of it we were broke, we were all freezing and just miserable, and we were crummy – the band was horrible. We were really an embarrassment – we didn't have amplifiers or anything. GEORGE

POST CARD

PRINTED IN ENGLAND

THIS IS A REAL PHOTOGRAPH

Dear Lou & Gordon,
I have been spending the week
in Inverness, so I thought
that you might like to
have another reminder of
the place. The Rock + Roll group
I am in, is Backing a well
known English rock star, around
this area, and we are doing 1
night stands at Dance Halls
We played at FORRES, Last night
and are at NEARN tonight.
Inverness hasn't changed. much
except for a few shops. We are
in the hotel on this card. I will
write write when I get home.
       LOVE GEORGE.

MR + MRS. G. CALDWELL.

KERR-ADDISON GOLD MINES,

VIRGINIATOWN

ONTARIO,

CANADA.

HAVE YOU
TAKEN OUT
YOUR LICENCE
FOR RADIO

57

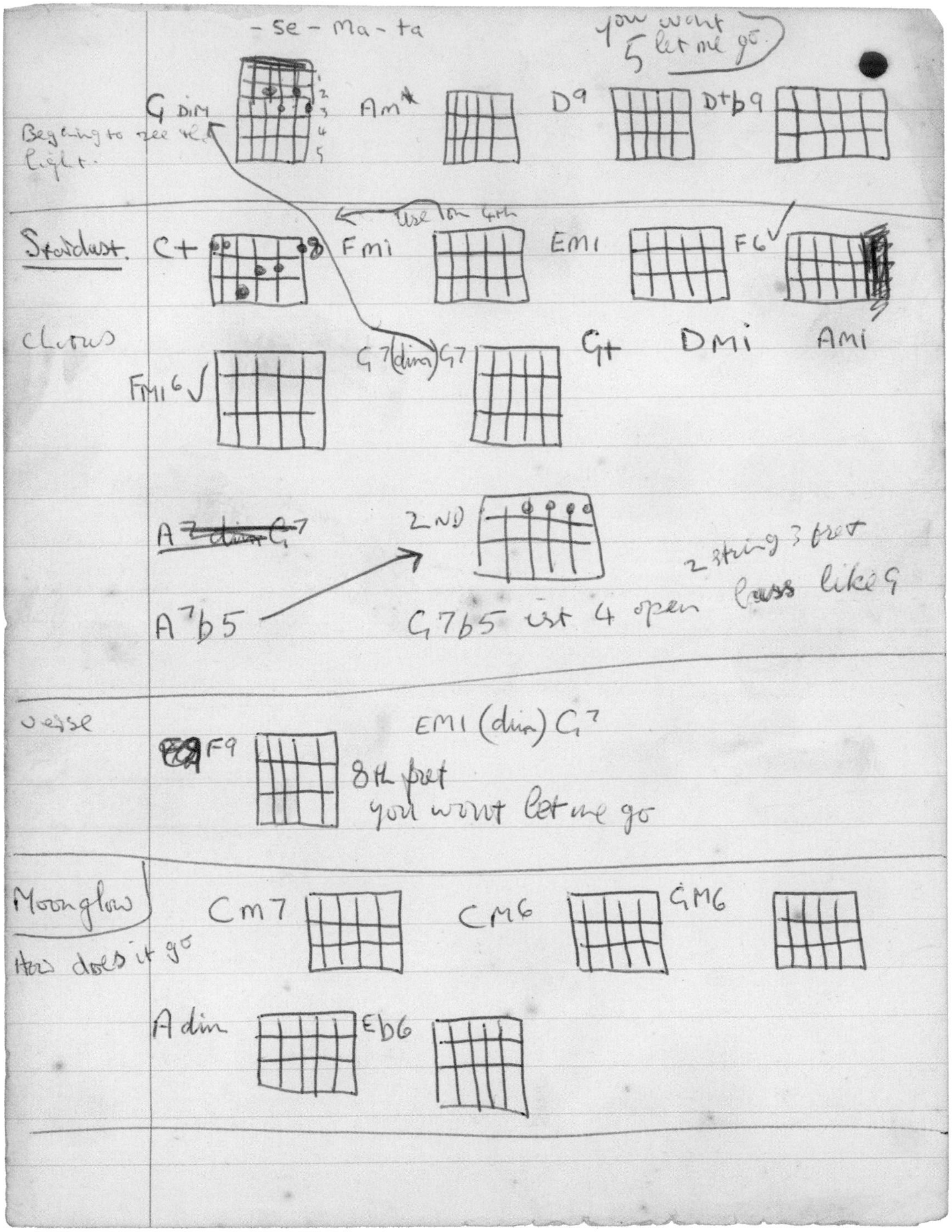

Pages from George's school exercise book, 1950s

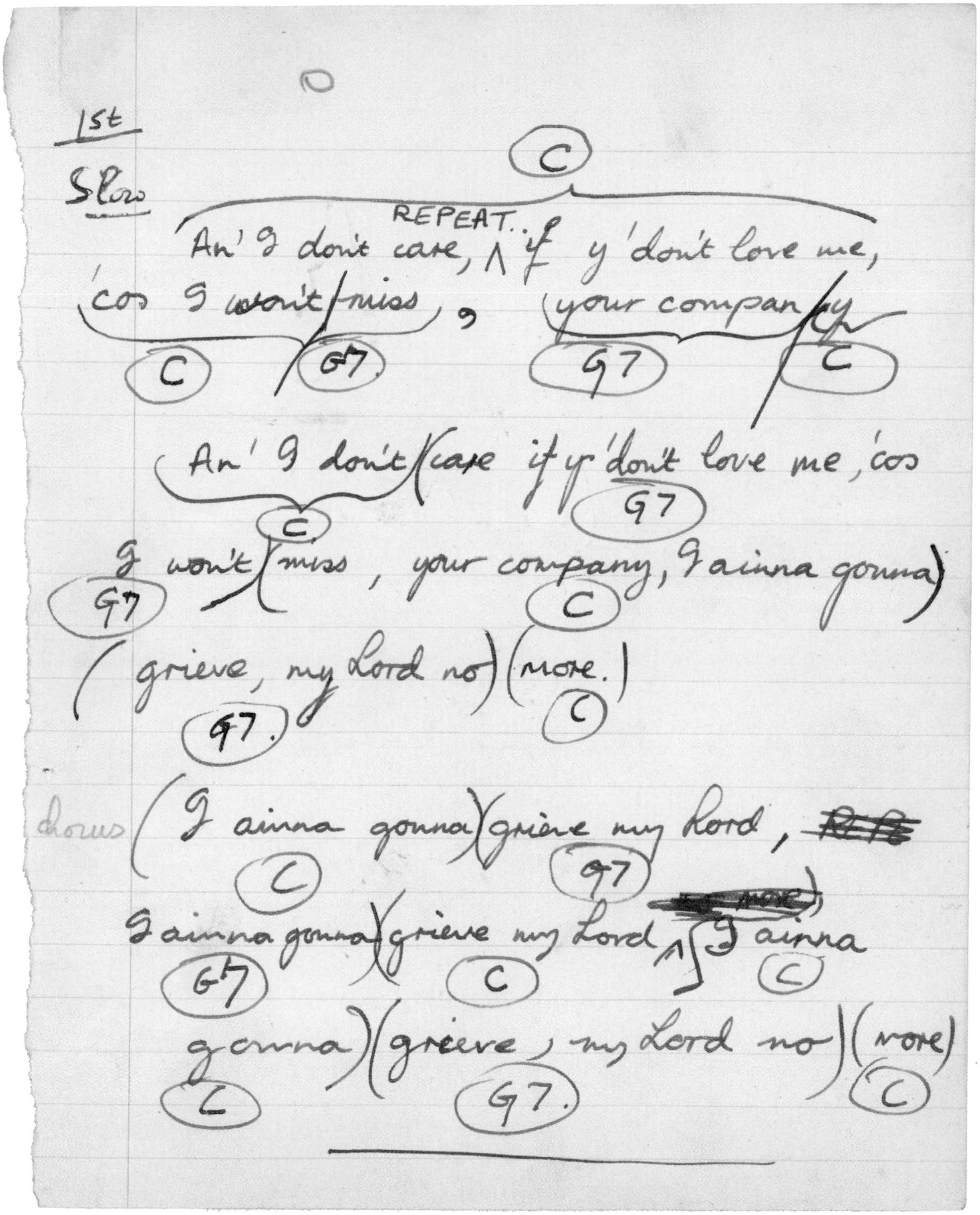

1st

Slow

C

REPEAT

An' I don't care, ^ if y' don't love me,
'cos I won't miss, your company
C G7 G7 C

An' I don't care if y' don't love me, 'cos
C G7

I won't miss, your company, I ainna gonna
G7 C

grieve, my Lord no more.
G7 C

chorus I ainna gonna grieve my Lord, ~~REP~~
C G7

I ainna gonna grieve my Lord ~~no more~~ ^ I ainna
G7 C C

gonna grieve, my Lord no more
C G7 C

George's autograph book, 1950s/60s

To George
Howdy...
es Paul

nixa RECORDS
LONNIE DONEGAN
78 r.p.m.

Putting On The Style
Gamblin' Man ... ...
Cumberland Gap ...
Love Is Strange
I'm Alabammy Bound
Don't You Rock Me Daddy-O
Dead or Alive ...
Bring A Little Water, Sylvie
Lost John
Stewball

N 15053
N 15087
N 15080
N 15071
N 15036

LONNIE DO
Lonnie Do
Wabash
Wre
F

Playing
oup

Lonnie Donegan

The Black Katz
Skiffle Group

Phone: CHI 2409.

97 Childwall Road,
Liverpool, 16.

Little
Richard
Virginia Rd.
Angeles, 19 Calif.

HARD

singt im
Star-Club
Hamburg-St. Pauli

61

A new club had opened in West Derby. We were only fifteen or sixteen and we just had to try this club out. The Casbah was in the cellar of a Victorian house, and the lighting was very dim. It was a coffee bar. No alcohol was sold, and I don't recall seeing anybody smoking in there. Sometimes they'd just play records on a big jukebox in the corner, but every so often they'd have groups, and one of the groups was the Quarrymen. Peter would give George a lift on his motorbike to the Casbah. I saw Peter there and I liked him, and we started courting from then on. But it was George that I knew first from playing in the group, when it was John, Paul, George and Ken Brown. Four guitarists who made a very different sound, something that was very raw and just got inside of you. It was a terrific sound. They drew huge crowds to the Casbah. It was jam-packed solid, maybe two hundred people in there. PAULINE HARRISON, *Sister-in-Law*

Poster for Casbah Promotions, 1961
Right, George and Paul, the Casbah Club, February 1961

They played Friday lunchtimes at the Cavern. I worked in Liverpool in the city centre, and the Cavern was not far away from where I worked. Their gig was from one o'clock until two o'clock, but if you wanted to get in you had to be there in plenty of time to get in that queue, so my friend and I would sneak away from work early and we'd never get back until at least ten-past two, and we got into trouble very frequently. It was impossible to leave before the end because it was so full in the Cavern. There, again, the acoustics in there made that raw sound. It just got into your whole body. They never quite caught on record the sound that was there at those performances in the Cavern and the Casbah. I can only think it was the acoustics there, and our excitement. PAULINE HARRISON

I knew Rory Storm when I was a young teenager – I think it was even before I met Paul and John – because I knew his sister Iris, and I think he had a skiffle group at that time. I remember thinking, 'That drummer, he's trouble. Gotta watch out for him.' And of course he turned out to be a big fan of us, and turned out to be our friend. Actually we were friendly with the lot of them, but Ringo was the special one. GEORGE

George, Rory Storm, Ringo, Johnny 'Guitar' Byrne and friends, Vi Caldwell's house, Liverpool, 1961
Right, George, Paul and Ringo, Vi Caldwell's house, Liverpool, 1961

When I first met The Beatles, I was with Rory Storm. George wasn't there actually – John and Paul were showing Stuart Sutcliffe how to play bass. They were just these lads. We had suits. You know what I mean? We, Rory and the Hurricanes, were like the top band in Liverpool, and we went to see these punks. We went our separate ways and then we met up again in Germany. RINGO STARR

When I met John he had a lot of power, really. Sometimes they pick somebody to march behind on the way to war – well, he was certainly out front.

When we got together, *The Beatles*, we had this amazing feeling of, 'We're going to do it.' We were just cocky. There was no justification for it – I don't know, just an inner feeling.
GEORGE

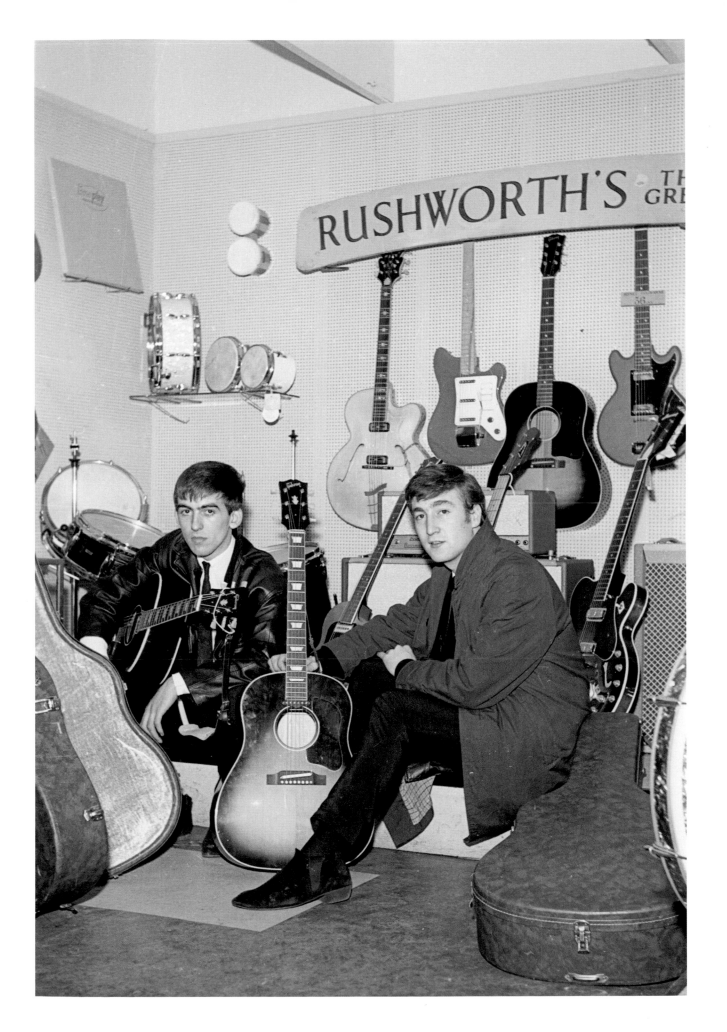

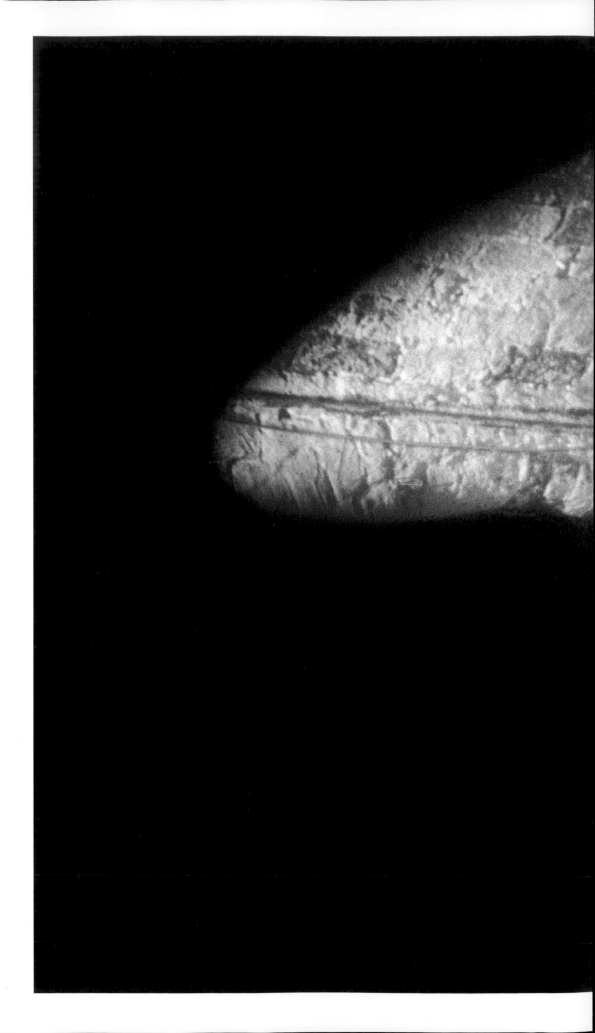

George, the Cavern Club, 1963
Pages 74–75, The Beatles, the Cavern Club, 1962

Left, Astrid Kirchherr, Cavern Club, 1964
Above, Brian Epstein, Cavern Club, early 1960s   77

78   George, Beatles' publicity shoot, Liverpool, 1962

2

Mach Schau

We didn't have that much money, we only just had enough to feed ourselves, so there was nothing really to show for it. But everything else was such a buzz, being right in the middle of the naughtiest city in the world, at seventeen years old.   GEORGE

Derry and the Seniors got offered this job to go to London. Allan Williams, who was the club owner who held the Larry Parnes' audition, drove them to London and got them a gig in the 2i's. So they were playing there and this fellow Bruno Koschmider, from this club in Hamburg, saw them and booked them to go to Germany. Then later he sent a message saying, 'I want another band,' probably because we were so cheap. So Allan Williams came to us and said, 'OK lads, you can have this job in Germany. The only problem is he's asked for a five-piece band.' At that point Paul was the drummer, because the drummers never showed up, and so that's when I said, 'I remember this guy Pete Best, he had a drum kit for Christmas. Let's find his number.' We gave him a call and he came down to the Jacaranda Club, we did a quick audition with him, and jumped in the van and went to Hamburg. GEORGE

We got into the city and were directed to the Reeperbahn, and it was fantastic because there were so many lights and clubs and bars; the whole place was lit up. It was exciting but at the same time we were in a foreign country and we'd got nowhere to stay and we didn't know where we were really going. Unfortunately the gig was way down this next street called Grosse Freiheit Strasse, right down the far end where all the coloured lights fizzled out and it turned back into just some kind of neighbourhood. And the place was called Indra, which for me is fascinating. It had two elephants in neon strung across the street. We played there and this club was kind of empty. He might have only just started it up and put us in there to get the club going. We caused a bit of noise and got banned because next door was a church – it seemed a bit of a strange place to have a church. So then he took us out and put us down in his other club, which was more where the lights were, down the street – the Kaiserkeller. Derry and the Seniors were just finishing off their gig there and he had Rory Storm and the Hurricanes booked in. He put us in there with Derry and the Seniors as well, and what he did was he gave them an hour, us an hour, them an hour, us an hour. So in effect if we were booked to play, say, four hours, we all had to be there for eight hours. On the weekends we were there all night, from like four in the afternoon till six in the morning.

We were given a lot of alcohol actually. If somebody liked the band, the waiter would suddenly show up on stage with some beers and he'd say, 'That's from these people at this table.' As things progressed somebody would come up with Schnapps or Sekt, which was German champagne. And I think it was on one of those weekends, where we were getting a bit merry and maybe starting to fall over a bit, that the manager of the club came to us and said, 'Why don't you have one of these, lads?' He gave us these pills which were called Preludin. We didn't know what they were – 'Sure, let's have one' – and suddenly we were back up on our feet again, singing! It got crazy.

Relative to what was happening in those days, Rory Storm and the Hurricanes were very professional. They all had good instruments, they had a full drum kit and they all had uniforms, matching ties and handkerchiefs. They had all the tunes put in a routine, a running order, and they did it like a show. Rory was out at the front, always trying to leap around and make a show – 'mach schau'. GEORGE

DESCRIPTION [2] SIGNALEMENT

	Bearer *Titulaire*	★Wife *Femme*
Profession *Profession*	STUDENT	MUSICIAN
Place and date of birth *Lieu et date* *de naissance*	ENGLAND 25/2/43	
Country of Residence *Pays de* *Résidence*	ENGLAND	
Height *Taille*	5 ft. 10 in.	ft. in.
Colour of eyes *Couleur des yeux*	BROWN	
Colour of hair *Couleur des cheveux*	BROWN	
Special peculiarities *Signes particuliers*	NONE	

★CHILDREN *ENFANTS*

Name *Nom*	Date of birth *Date de naissance*	Sex *Sexe*

Usual signature of bearer
Signature du titulaire   *George Harrison*

Usual signature of wife
Signature de sa femme _____

3

Bearer
Titulaire

Wife
Femme

Hamburg, 1960s
Pages 88–89, A display case in the Star Club, Hamburg, 1960s

It was after wartime – you still had lots of bombed houses, lots of derelict places. Not poverty – the Germans were rich quite quick. It didn't take them long to pick up on that one. But the harbour was bombed badly.

The Reeperbahn is the red-light district in Hamburg. The Reeperbahn is really for the sailors, for people getting drunk, for people going to see naked women or people having sex, or whatever. That's what this place is known for.

I first saw the band when I was working as a commercial artist and I went down the Reeperbahn. I was just walking around and I heard this band playing in a basement. And the first band that I ever heard was The Beatles actually. I went into the club. There were lots of rockers around, and I was really shit-scared, I must admit. It was in the basement. And that just knocked me out. It was beautiful.

That particular day I'd had an argument with Astrid and I was really wired up and I was angry and wanted to let steam off. And I quite often went in that direction, all the way through St Pauli, Reeperbahn and down to the harbour. Sometimes I went to a cinema or I just went for a walk. On that particular day I went past the basement and heard that particular band.

They didn't have the leather gear yet. Maybe John had a leather jacket on already. But the leather thing came when they met Astrid and me and the way we were. When we first met them they were more like Teddy boys. And it really went off like fireworks. They not only made sound, but created this whole feeling on stage. They were communicating with each other. I was just completely drawn in, and it changed my whole life. We loved this band. They were so fantastic. KLAUS VOORMANN, *Artist, musician and friend*

Klaus was always very laid-back; you couldn't quite impress him with things. But when he came home after seeing The Beatles for the first time, I've never seen him like that before, he just went crazy. When I came down to the Kaiserkeller with Klaus, after he had to persuade me for three days, I just freaked out seeing them on stage. Faces I always dreamed of taking pictures of, because they had so much personality and were still young, like I was. ASTRID KIRCHHERR, *Photographer and friend*

war, weil der Lindenbaum Laube hatte
10). Der Reiter wusste dass jemand in dem Baum war, weil er zwei Beine sah.

~~~~~~~~

1). Der Taugenichts hielt den Atem um besser hören zu können und lauschte
2). Die Pferde schnaubten weil sie gelaufen werden
3). Sie sprachen so dass niemand anders sie hören könnten
4). Der Lindenbaum stand am Rande des Waldes.
5). Er streckte sich lang' aus so dass er den Baum steigen konnte.
6).

7). Nein, die Reiter steigen nicht von den Pferden ab
8). Der Taugenichts drückte die Augenfest zu weil er erschrecken war.
9). Ich wisse das es Sommer

George was only seventeen years of age. And in one way I thought he was just a little boy, but in another way, interestingly enough now after all these years, you realise that he was more mature then the rest. He was calm. He looked you straight in the face. KLAUS VOORMANN

Pages from George's German vocabulary school notebook, 1950s
Right, Self-portrait, c. 1960
Pages 94–95, John, George, Pete Best, Paul and Stuart Sutcliffe on stage at the Indra, Hamburg, 1960

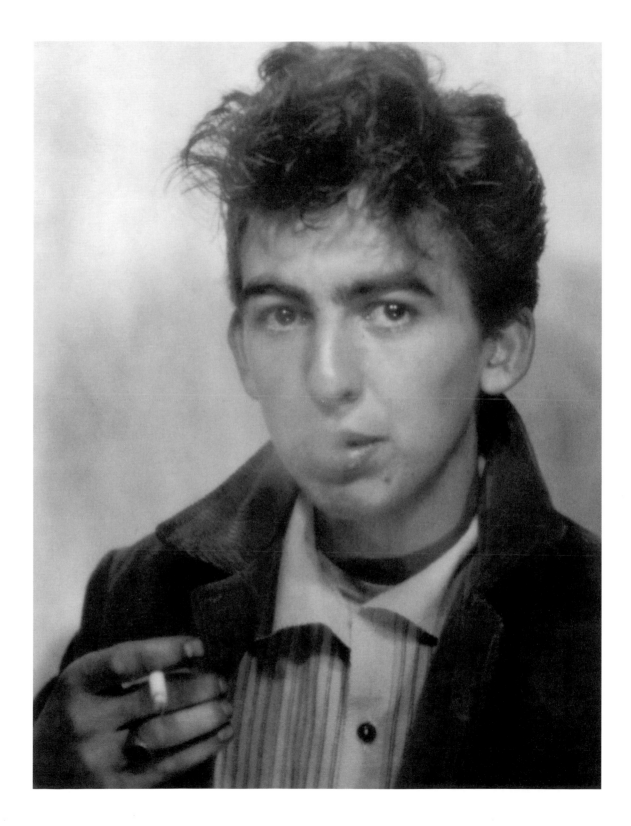

The Beatles, the Star Club, Hamburg, 1962
Right, The Star Club, Hamburg, 1962

98   The Star Club, Hamburg, 1962

They lived in these rooms you wouldn't believe. The room they stayed in first in the Bambi Kino was the sort of place where you would normally put brooms and things. There was just the lightbulb on the ceiling. No wardrobe. No washing room. They were living in these little cupboards, so to speak, right behind this little cinema. They had to go for their morning wash after playing all night. They'd get up about two or three o'clock and they met the customers who were already watching those movies in the front. Astrid was just like heaven for them. She took them to her house and she cooked for them. Her mother was cooking their favourite meals for them. They even got English food. They would be scrubbed up and have their hair washed. KLAUS VOORMANN

As kids, there was so much good to it, being there, that we didn't care about the bad side really. It was a bit messy, having to sleep in a room full of sweaty men and boys, with John and everybody all huddled together. There was no bathroom or anything, but then we'd had practice because we didn't have a bathroom at home in Arnold Grove. That side of it was a bit messy. GEORGE

George in his bedroom at Upton Green, Liverpool, 1960, from George's camera

Right, Reverse of photo on p102

This is taken with a flash camera
I bought. It is me sitting on
my bed in our room. My
shirt on the wall, [to save you
puzzling]!!

C529

love

George

He went out to Hamburg a little boy and came back all grown up. It made a huge difference to him. He went out with a parting and his hair down, and came back with it spiked up and his leathers and his cowboy boots. I just realised that nobody's ever going to tell him what to do any more, because he'd experienced too much out there. They'd had to look after themselves. IRENE HARRISON

Above and Right, Paul, John and George on the roof of the Top Ten Club, Hamburg, 1961, from George's camera

George with his guitars at the Top Ten Club, Hamburg, 1961

The Beatles with Little Richard, the Tower Ballroom, New Brighton, Liverpool, 1962

Right before we went back to Hamburg, Brian Epstein hired Little Richard to do a gig at the Liverpool Empire, and put us on the bill. So, by the time we got to Hamburg we'd already met Richard, briefly. GEORGE

I looked at these four guys and thought, 'Well, none of them shines as being above all the others,' and I had to make up my mind, in my silly mind, who the lead singer was going to be. Suddenly I realised I would take them as they were, as a group. The hell with a lead singer. They would be singing together. GEORGE MARTIN

George during The Beatles' first official recording session, EMI, Abbey Road, 1962
Right, The Beatles during their first official recording session, EMI, Abbey Road, 1962

Tel: MIDland 8171

ALBANY HOTEL SMALLBROOK BIRMINGHAM 5

<u>SATURDAY JUNE 29th.</u>

Dear Lou,
      Sorry I have been so
long before replying, but I dont
get much time nowadays to do
anything normal.
      First of all thanks for your
letter, and I have arranged for
our music publisher to send
about 1 dozen copies of 'From me to
you', so they should reach you
shortly after this letter. They will
have the British Parlophone label on
with something like "VEE-JAY FOR U.S.A"
stuck over it, so they should be O.K.
We can't do anything about that,
      and we must have our records

Telegraphic Address : ALBANY, BIRMINGHAM Telex : 33703

②

released through the E.M.I.
outlets in the U.S, so thats
why we are on VEE-JAY. Still
I believe it is quite a good
company and they do have a lot
of Hit records on that label.
Well now as I have got that bit
over with I dont know where to
begin, as there are so many things
to tell you.
1/. We will be topping the Bill on
the London Palladium in September,
which is nearly everybodys professional
ambition.
2/. Our long playing record has been
(and still is) Nº 1 in the L.P.
charts. Incidentally, it has sold more
copies in Gt. Britain than anything
else since South Pacific soundtrack.
(How about that!)

Left, George backstage, Granada Cinema, East Ham, London, 1963
Above, George's letter to his sister, Louise Caldwell, 1963   113

George and Roy Orbison backstage whilst on tour together, England, 1963
Right, George's letter to his sister, Louise Caldwell, 1963

Tel: MIDland 8171

ALBANY HOTEL SMALLBROOK BIRMINGHAM 5

3) We make our next record on Monday, called 'She Loves You'. By the way do you mind if Ringo and I pop over to see you all at the end of September? I'm not joking, we are having another 2 weeks holiday, (the definate dates are not yet fixed,) so I thought of flying over to see everybody, and maybe call in at Nashville for a few days too, to see Roy Orbison (whom we met on tour over here) and possibly Chet Atkins a favourite of mine, if we have time.

I will come on my own if Ringo doesn't come, but I think he will as he wants to see the States as well.

This letter doesn't seem to make sense but don't worry too much about it because it is quite late, and I'm tired, and it took some courage to think 'I'll go to bed later' believe me!

Remember me to Gordon, and give my love to Gordon Jr. and Lesley, Cheerio love from

George (Brother?)

(P.S.)

I am buying a new car soon, possibly a Jaguar.

(Big head!)

George was the best guitarist in the group. I mean, we were all pretty good, but George was lead guitar. John would take turns because John was good too. He had a more primitive style, but George was more technical, more practical, and we all thought he was a great guitar player. The nice thing was that he didn't really emulate anyone. There wasn't the Jimi Hendrixes and the Claptons to emulate, there was just a lot of people. Eddie Cochran was great, we loved Eddie; Buddy Holly was great; so we had a few heroes. But George built his own style out of that. PAUL McCARTNEY

George's Gretsch guitar, Abbey Road Studios, during recording sessions for 'Don't Bother Me'/*With The Beatles*, 1963
Right, George Martin, Abbey Road Studios, during recording sessions for 'Don't Bother Me'/*With The Beatles*, 1963

Above and Right, George with his Gretsch guitar, recording vocals, during recording sessions for 'Don't Bother Me'/*With The Beatles* at Abbey Road, 1963

Pages 120–21, Sign for The Beatles, Trini Lopez and Sylvie Vartan Show, the Olympia, Paris, 1964, photograph by George

Paul, Hotel George V, Paris, 1964, photograph by George

Right, John, Hotel George V, Paris, 1964, photograph by George

Pages 124–25, John on board The Beatles' first flight to the USA, 1964, photograph by George

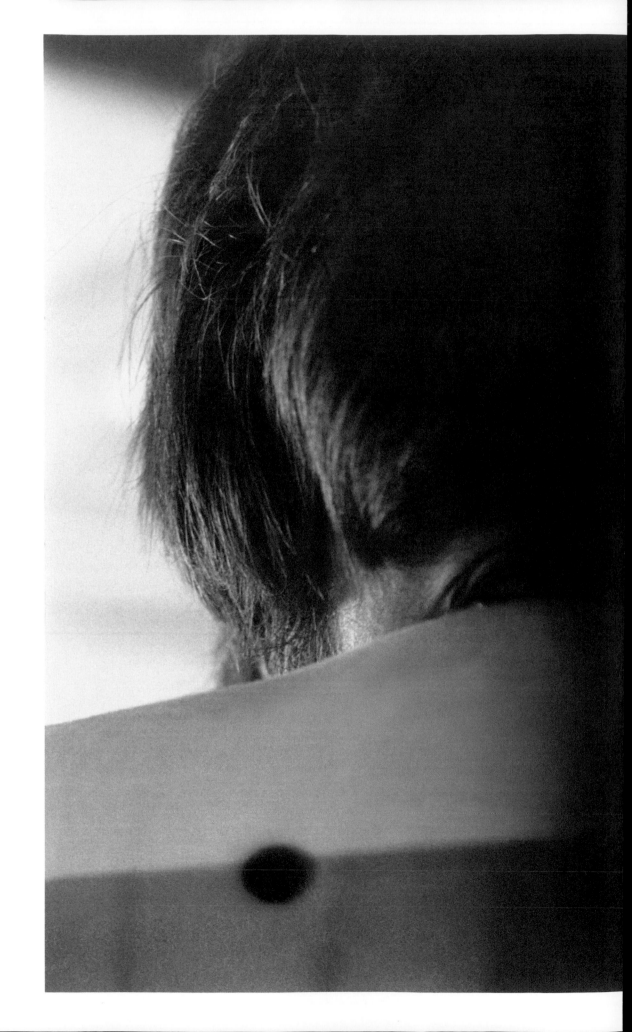

Phil Spector on board The Beatles' first flight to the USA, 1964, photograph by George
Right, John, Paris, 1964, photograph by George
Pages 128–29, Clay busts of The Beatles by sculptor David Wynne, modelled in the Hotel George V, Paris, 1964, photograph by George

130 Self-portrait (double exposure), Paris, 1964

131

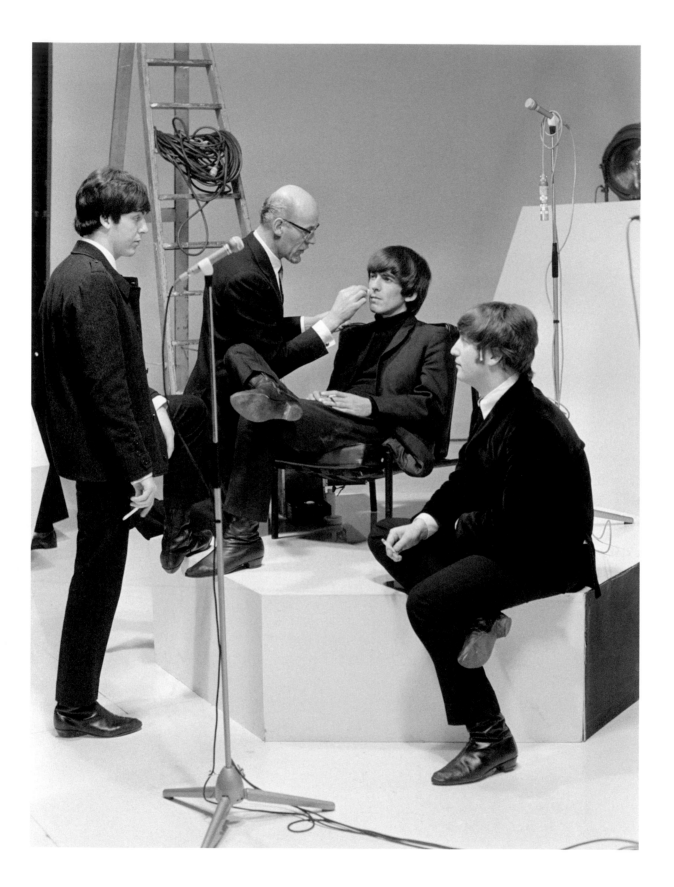

We were always a little nervous before each step we went up the ladder, but we always had that confidence, and that was the good thing about being four together. I always felt sorry later for Elvis, because he was on his own, nobody else knew what he felt like. But for us, we all shared the experience. GEORGE

The Beatles performing, 1963

3

A Puff
of Madness

The mania side of it started happening in 1963, when we began touring seriously in England. And then we did some tours around Europe, and I think it was because of the mania that was happening then that the Americans caught on – they did features on us in *Time* and *Life* and *Newsweek*. That set us up for the trip to the USA in 1964. The mania got to me in 1966, and around that time I got a bit tired of what they call the adulation. I'm still not that keen on that side of it. It's nice to be popular. It's nice to be loved. But it's not so nice to be chased around and on the front page of the paper every day of your life, with people climbing over the wall all day long.   GEORGE

George and Manhattan skyline, Liberty Island, 1963, from George's camera

Roof terrace in midtown Manhattan, 1963, from George's camera
Right, Empire State Building, New York, 1963, from George's camera
Pages 142–43, Paul, John, Mal Evans and others on flight from Hong Kong to Australia, The Beatles' World Tour, 1964, photograph by George
Pages 144–45, Arrival of The Beatles, Darwin airstrip, Australia, 1964, photograph by George
Pages 146–47, Adelaide airport, Australia, 1964, photograph by George
Pages 148–53, The Beatles' motorcade to Adelaide, 1964, photographs by George

George always seemed to have a camera with him. He took a lot of 8 mm footage too, from the time he went to visit his sister in America in 1963.   OLIVIA HARRISON

SHERATON
MOTOR HOTEL
40 MACLEAY STREET, POTTS POINT
SYDNEY, N.S.W.

THE
KEY HOTEL
OF SYDNEY

Dear Mum and Dad,

We have been and played at the Stadium here in Sydney, and it was the biggest drag of all time. The stage revolves once every 3 minutes, and we have to walk right down the aisle (like the boxers) to get on the stage. At first house, I punched a policeman because he was shoving me like mad, and some kids had hold of me all at once, as I was trying to get off the stage. It was awful, and the Police havent ever had it before, so they panic and just

Letter from George in Sydney to his parents, 1964
Right, Letter from George in Adelaide to his parents, 1964

Pages 156–57, John and Paul on balcony, Australia, 1964, photograph by George

SOUTH AUSTRALIAN HOTEL PTY. LIMITED
ADELAIDE

12th/June.

Dear Mum and Dad,

We have just arrived in Adelaide, and
the crowds were ridiculous. We drove at about
5 M.P.H. all the way from the Airport to
the Town Hall, and people lined the roads
all the way into town. When we
got to the Town Hall, we had to make
an appearance on the balcony, and all.
The street was blocked with the crowd
I took a lot of pictures of the
crowds and have sent the roll off to
the Daily Express, so if they use any
of the photographs, then it should be
the photo news on Monday or Tuesday.

①

155

158   The Beatles arriving on stage, 1964

The Beatles on stage at ABC Cinema (aka the Apollo),
Manchester, 1963

Fame changes all really. It's great in the beginning when you are recognised, you get a great seat in the restaurant, and things are bigger and things come to you faster. All that is great. And then you really want that to end. It can get a little scary, and it never ends. That's the deal.   RINGO STARR

One of the very earliest interviews we did, it must have been 1963, every time I look at it, I think it looks as though I'd had my brain removed before I did the interview – sometimes it still feels like that! But even in 1963 in this interview what I'm saying was that you look in the paper and you see them talking about Paul McCartney and John Lennon, Ringo Starr and George Harrison but you just read it as if it's somebody else. And I think that for me has been a good point throughout all this madness: I see it as somebody else. You know Beatles are something else quite apart from me, and this thing of being Beatle George – I'm not really Beatle George. I'm sorry to disappoint you, but that is just a little part that got played through in this life, I mean there is much more to me than the Beatle George.   GEORGE

us very welcome. Tonight we were invited to Burt Lancasters house to see the new Peter Sellers film 'A Shot in the dark' and Paul and I went. He was great, just like in the films, and we enjoyed the film. After that the men from General Artistes (who are organising the tour, wanted us to go to this place called 'Whiskey a Go Go' on Sunset Strip and they said it would be great and we wouldn't be bothered.

Got there and went in and fought our way (with Mal and a few big hard men) to a table where John and Derek were and Jayne Mansfield.

By this time, after fighting through the crowd I was annoyed and I threw some coke on a camera man

2

Above and Right, Letter from George in Los Angeles, 1964
166   *Far Right*, George, Ringo and John with Jayne Mansfield, the Whisky a Go Go, Hollywood, Los Angeles, 1964

After that we all fought
our way back out, and jumped
in a car and went home. It
was a drag and we were in there
for about 10 minutes altogether
   You see why we dont usually
bother going out now, because
its no fun, and soft gits
like Mansfield Try and get a
bit of publicity out of us.
   Col. Tom Parker, Elvis's manager
came to see us and gave us all
real leather belts and holster
sets (Cowboy things) and little
covered wagons which are television
lamps. He was good too, and
said Elvis wants to meet us, and
has invited us to his house in
Memphis Tennessee, but we wont
be able to go, I dont think.

3

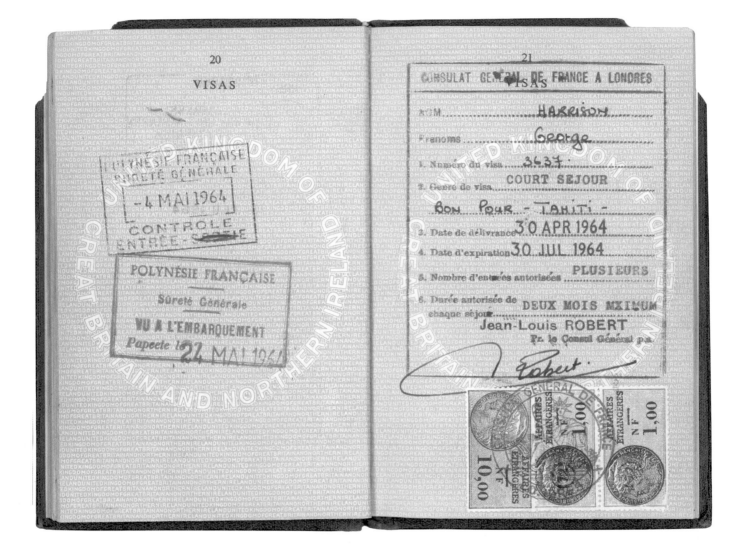

George's passport, 1964

Right, John, Tahiti, 1964, photograph by George

I woke and looked out of the porthole. It was fantastic. At that time we'd hardly been anywhere out of England, and never to anywhere that was tropical. It was incredible, a smooth lagoon with the island in the background with mountains and coconut palms. Five or six Tahitians were paddling an outrigger canoe, gliding across the calm sea. It blissed me out. GEORGE

George, Bora Bora, 1964, from George's camera

Right, George, Tahiti, 1964, from George's camera

Above and Right, Fans on the beach outside the Deauville Hotel, Miami, Florida, 1964, photograph by George
Pages 174–75, Message from fans on the beach outside the Deauville Hotel, Miami, Florida, 1964, photograph by George

I quit the band on the 'White Album'. I was just in some emotional state where I honestly felt I wasn't playing well, and those three were really close, and I thought, 'Well, I've got to deal with this.' So I went over to John, who was staying with Yoko in my apartment, and I said, 'Look man, I've got to say, I feel I'm not playing really good and you three are really close.' And he goes, '*I thought it was you three.*' And I went to Paul's and I knocked on his door and he said the same thing, 'I thought it was you three.' And I thought, 'Oh shit, I'm going on holiday.' And that's when I left. And then I was getting telegrams. They said, 'Come on back, we love you.' And the other side of George: when I got back, George had decorated the whole studio with flowers, and that was a beautiful moment for me.   RINGO STARR

David Frost:
How do you come to reach this stage of meditation?

George Harrison:
Each person's individual life pulsates in a certain rhythm, so they give you a word or a sound, known as a mantra, which pulsates with that rhythm. The whole idea is to transcend to the subtlest level of thought, so you replace the thought with the mantra, and the mantra becomes more and more subtle until finally you've lost even the mantra. Then you find yourself at that level of pure consciousness.

David Frost:
Is the mantra something you use to get back to the subject if you find earthly or irrelevant thoughts intruding?

John Lennon:
Yes, it's sort of like that. You just sort of sit there and you let your mind go. It doesn't matter what you're thinking about, just let it go, and then you just introduce the mantra or the vibration to take over from the thought. You don't will it, or use your willpower.

George Harrison:
We've only been doing it for a matter of six weeks, and there's definite proof I've had that it is something that really works. But in actual fact it'll take a long time to arrive at the point where I'm able to bring that level of consciousness into this level of consciousness, which is the aim of it.

DAVID FROST, GEORGE HARRISON AND JOHN LENNON
in conversation on 'The Frost Programme', 29 September 1967

1
SATURDAY

Recorded Sgt. Peppers Lonely-Hearts club-band-part 2

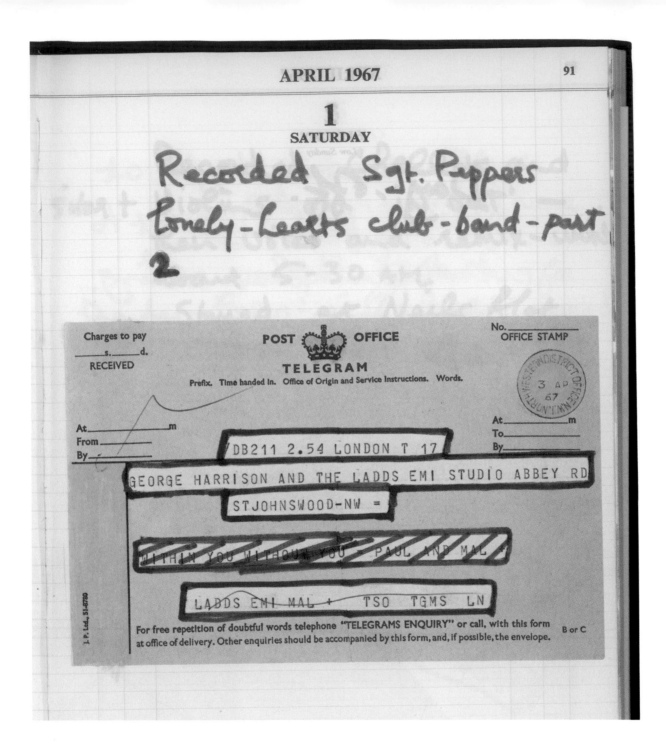

The non-stop change was amazing. As it's happening, you don't think about it. I mean, when I got out of school all I wanted to do was be in a band. I didn't want a proper job, and I had no idea what I would have done had I not done this. But at the age of seventeen I was in Hamburg, in St Pauli, and by the time I was twenty-three we had done *Sgt. Pepper* and I was in the Himalayas. Every experience was great. It was speeded up. We put in maybe twenty years in every year, just in experience.   GEORGE

Page from George's diary, 1967

Right, George painting murals on the Esher house, 1967

George chose to move into a house in Esher, maybe eight miles north of where I was born. We became friends and I would go visit them there and something grew out of the music and the kind of people we were. I think we shared a lot of tastes too, superficial things – cars or clothes, and women obviously – but I think what George might have liked about me was the fact that I was kind of a free agent. I think he may have already been wondering about whether he was in the right place being in a group, because the group politic is a tricky one. There was a lot about what he had going which I envied, and there was a lot about what I had going that he envied. ERIC CLAPTON

George's Mini Cooper S, from George's camera

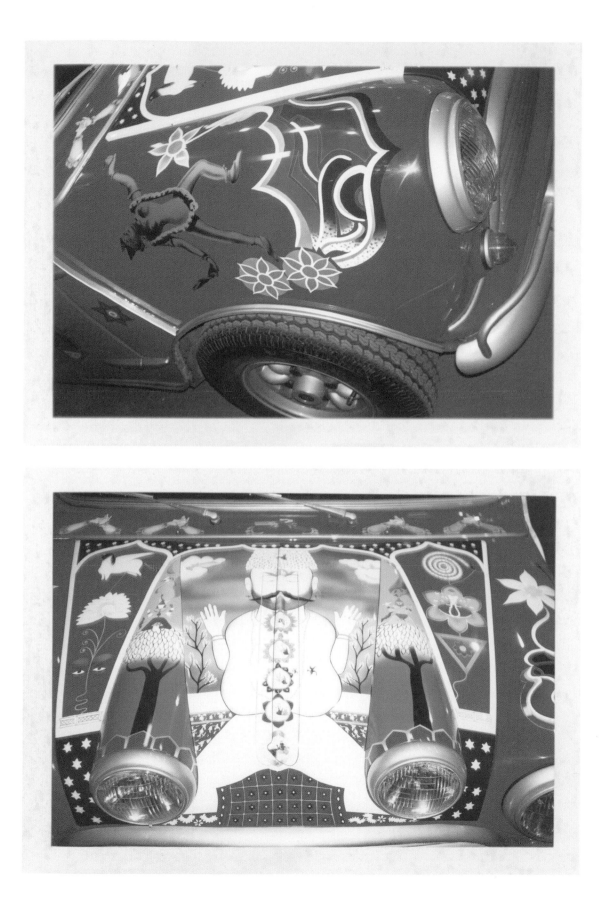

LSD was just like opening the door – and before, you didn't even know that there was a door there. It opened up this whole other consciousness and awareness, even if it was down to, like Huxley said, the wonderful folds in his great flannel trousers, to the fact that every blade of grass and every grain of sand is just throbbing and pulsating.

I had this lingering thought that just stayed with me after that, and that thought was 'Yogis of the Himalayas'. I don't know why – I'd never thought about them for the rest of my life, but suddenly this thought was in the back of my consciousness. It was like somebody was whispering to me: 'Yogis of the Himalayas'. GEORGE

George, at home in front of fireplace painted by The Fool, 1967

10 FRIDAY

Got up went to Twickenham rehearsed until lunch time - left the Beatles - went home and in the Evening did King of Fuh at Trident Studio - had chips later at Klaus and Christines went home.

DECEMBER 1968

S	1	8	15	22	29	·
M	2	9	16	23	30	·
T	3	10	17	24	31	·
W	4	11	18	25	·	·
T	5	12	19	26	·	·
F	6	13	20	27	·	·
S	7	14	21	28	·	·

JANUARY 1969

S	·	5	12	19	26	·
M	·	6	13	20	27	·
T	·	7	14	21	28	·
W	1	8	15	22	29	·
T	2	9	16	23	30	·
F	3	10	17	24	31	·
S	4	11	18	25	·	·

Got up - John and Yoko came
and diverted me at Breakfast

He was clearly an innovator: George, to me, was taking certain elements of R&B and rock and rockabilly and creating something unique. I had quite a lot of self-confidence going in my concept of myself as a sort of blues missionary, and I wasn't looking for any favours from anybody. And George recognised me as an equal because I had a level of proficiency even then that he saw as being fairly unique too.

In the early days, what was good about being George's friend was that it was kind of like basking in the sunshine of this immense creativity. Whenever we were together in public, for all the amount of weight that I thought I carried, I would turn into nobody. If we were going into a restaurant or a club, the way people would behave around The Beatles' aura was beyond belief. ERIC CLAPTON

In the Sixties there was a period when I started playing the sitar and hanging out with Ravi Shankar, and I took some lessons for a couple of years. After that period I thought, well, I've got to get back, because really I'm a pop person, right? I'm neglecting the guitar and what I'm supposed to do, and I'm never going to be a brilliant sitar player – because I had already met a thousand of them in India, and Ravi thought only one of them was going to make it as a really top-class sitar player. I still play the sitar now for my own amusement. But I thought I'd better get back on the guitar, and by that time there was all these people who were playing brilliantly. I thought, I'm so out of touch I don't even know how to get a half-decent sound.

What happened was I went on this tour with Delaney and Bonnie. They had a record out, *Delaney and Bonnie and Friends*, and Dave Mason had played slide guitar on the record. So Delaney said, 'Here's the slide and you play the Dave Mason part,' and I said, 'Oh, I don't play the slide.' But after that I thought, 'Well, maybe I'll try.' So I started to play slide. GEORGE

Bob Dylan on television, photograph by George

Right, George with Bob and Sara Dylan, Woodstock, New York, 1968, from George's camera

Bob Dylan and George photographed by Jill Krementz in Woodstock, 1968

Above and Right, George and Bob Dylan during the Isle of Wight Festival, 1969, from George's camera

I don't mean to embarrass Bob or anything like that, but he's said and done more, I think, than the lot of show business put together. You can take just one tune from back in the Sixties and it's more meaningful than twenty or thirty years of what everybody else said, and yet he's cranked out so many of them and said it with such insight and such wit — because that's the thing that I pick up from him, he's really funny. And I suppose in a way he's a hero of mine. But, at the same time, like with Ravi, I'm blessed in as much as being with them just makes life that much better. GEORGE

We'd been through every race riot, and every city we went to there was some kind of a jam going on, and police control, and people threatening to do this or that, and just travel and the intensity and the noise, and people yelling at us all the time, and being confined to a little room or a plane or a car. We all had each other to dilute the stress, and the sense of humour was very important, so we always you know had a laugh as well. But there was a point where enough was enough. GEORGE

4

Pilgrimage

Each person has to find for himself a way for inner realisation. I still believe that's the only reason we're on this planet. It's like going to school again: each soul is potentially divine and the goal is to manifest that divinity. Everything else is secondary.   GEORGE

Self-portrait, Kashmir, 1966

Ravi Shankar with Shambhu Das and Pattie Boyd, Kashmir, 1966, photograph by George

Right, Kashmir, 1966, photograph by George

Kailash Temple, Ellora, India, 1966, photograph by George
Right, Ajanta caves, Maharashtra, India, 1966, photograph by George

214   *Above and Right*, Street scenes, India, 1966, photographs by George

I could meet anybody. I could go in all the film stars' houses and meet Elvis and everybody, and we met a lot of really good people, but I never met one person who really impressed me. The first person who ever impressed me in my life was Ravi Shankar, and he was the only person who didn't try to impress me.

Ravi Shankar, India, 1966, photograph by George
Right, George, India, 1966, from George's camera

Pages 218–19, Sitar lesson, Srinagar, India, 1966, from George's camera

If you're trying to find something, to find the source of that thing is very difficult, but my blessing was to be able to have Ravi as my patch cord, and he could plug me in to the real thing. So my experience of it was always the best quality. GEORGE

Ravi and the sitar was like an excuse, trying to find the spiritual connection. I read stuff by various holy men and swamis and mystics, and I went around and looked for them. Ravi and his brother Raju gave me a lot of books by some wise men. One of the books was by Swami Vivekananda, who said, 'If there's a God we must see him and if there's a soul we must perceive it. Otherwise it's better not to believe. It's better to be an outspoken atheist than a hypocrite.'

There was a period in India where I first went out there and I started rigorously practising – it was all the very early stages, exercises and scales and suchlike – and at that point I was listening to a lot of music, going to a lot of concerts and watching a lot of Ravi's other students practising.

I wasn't intending to try and be a great sitar player; I just wanted to learn how to play it, learn a bit more about it.

What impressed me was he said that he felt like he'd only just started, and that realisation that no matter how great you are, how big you are, there is always something else to know, there's always more to come. GEORGE

India was the first foreign country I ever went to. I never felt Denmark or Holland or France were foreign, just the language was different, but when you got to India it was very hard to know what the hell was going on. Over the years, I got to love the music myself and now I'm a Christian Hindu with Buddhist tendencies. Thanks to George, who opened my eyes as much as anyone else's. RINGO STARR

Left, Lord Ganesh poster, Annette Funicello and Paul Anka poster, Madras, India, 1976, photograph by George
Above, Ringo, John, George and Paul on a stopover, India, July, 1966   223

Ringo, John and Paul, India, 1966, photograph by George
Right, India, 1966, photograph by George

DEHRA - DUN

Chorus / Dehra - Dehra Dun - Dehra Dun - Dun
Dehra Dehra Dun - Dehra Dun Dun
Dehra - Dehra Dun - Dehra - Dun Dun - Dehra
                                                    Dehra - Dun.

① Many Roads can take you there
Many different ways,,
One direction takes you years, another
takes you days.
        chorus

②   ~~Many~~ many People on the Roads, looking
at the sights,, ~~Meeting Strangers~~ Many OTHERS, with their ~~coming~~
troubles looking for their Rights.
chorus.   H - K - L - M - N - P
                                           S

③ See them move along the Road
in Search of Life Divine —
unaware its all around them
Beggars in a Goldmine —
        chorus.

Maureen Starkey, Jane Asher, Paul McCartney, Maharishi Mahesh Yogi, George and Pattie Boyd, Rishikesh, 1968, from George's camera
Pages 230–31, Paul, Cynthia and John, Rishikesh, India, 1968, photograph by George

I had a strange experience when I was in Rishikesh. I went on a meditation course, where the object was to meditate deeper and deeper and deeper for long periods, and the goal was really to plug into the divine energy and to raise your state of consciousness and tune into the subtler states of consciousness. So it's hard to actually explain it, but it was a feeling of just the consciousness travelling. I don't know where to, and it wasn't up, down, left or right, but there was no body there, and at the same time you don't feel as though you're missing anything. The consciousness is complete.

I have this kind of strange thing, and I put it down to being a Pisces. Pisces is the sign of two fish. The way I see it is that one half is going where the other half has just been. I was in the West and I was into rock 'n' roll, getting crazy, staying up all night and doing whatever were supposed to be the wrong things. That's in conflict with all the right things, which is what I learned through India – like getting up early, going to bed early, taking care of yourself and having some sort of spiritual quality to your life. I've always had this conflict.   GEORGE

The Hare Krishna mantra is at least 5,000 years old and probably quite a bit older than that. The words are names of God and God's consort. Hare is sometimes called Radha. The value of chanting the mantra is to have communion with God, to have a direct, personal association.

George took on this project himself to record the devotees singing the Hare Krishna mantra. It was quite amazing because none of us thought this was going to be a popular record, and yet it became very popular. I think it was played in the intermission at the Isle of Wight concert when Bob Dylan was setting up, in the summer of 1969. And it was played at the intermission in a football game at Manchester United, and all the fans who were just there to watch the soccer started singing along with it. Thousands of football fans singing Hare Krishna. That was another way to say that the mantra had penetrated the British society. MUKUNDA GOSWAMI, *Early disciple of A.C. Bhaktivedanta Swami Prabhupada*

238   George and Hare Krishna devotees recording the *Radha Krishna Temple* album, London, 1969

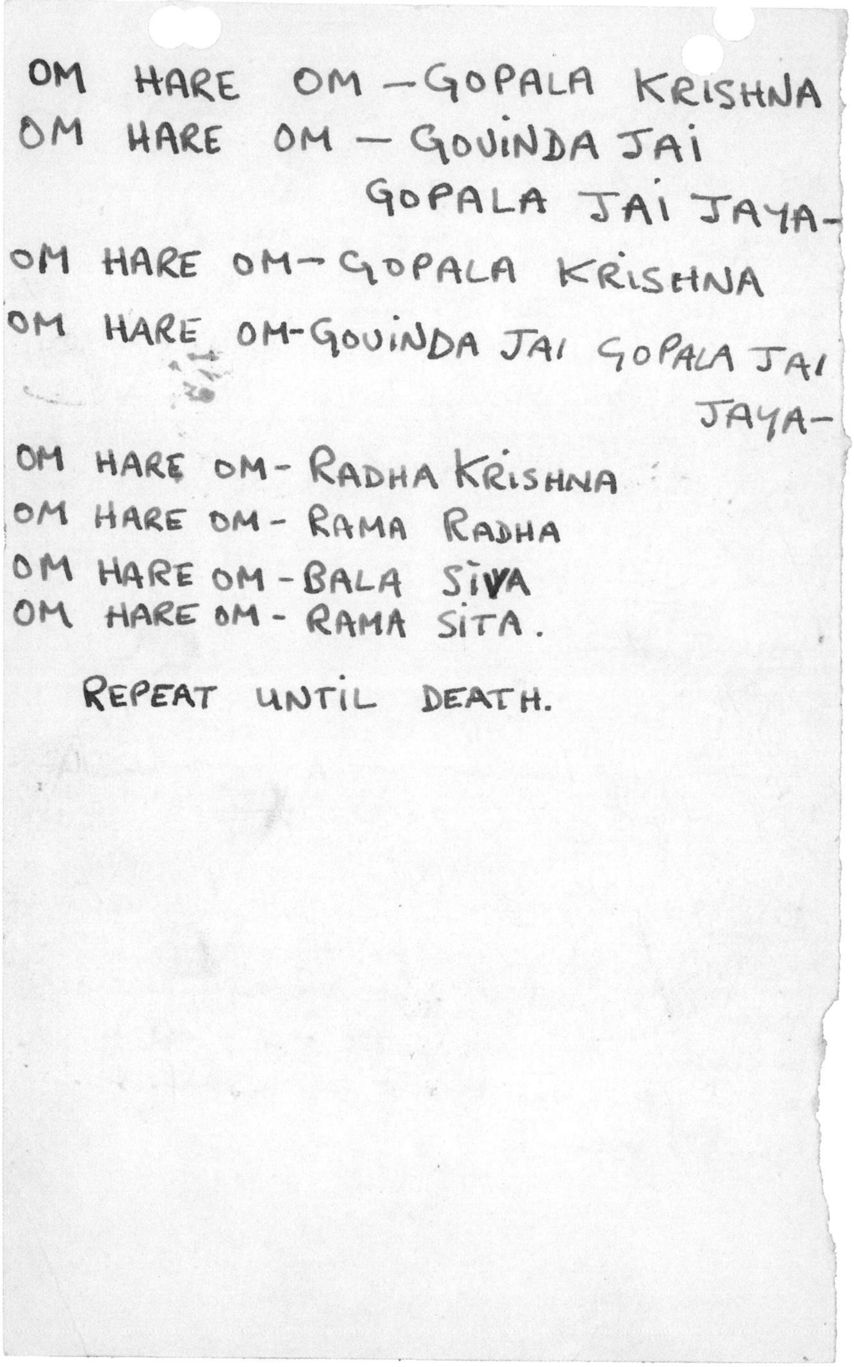

OM HARE OM — GOPALA KRISHNA
OM HARE OM — GOVINDA JAI
                    GOPALA JAI JAYA —
OM HARE OM — GOPALA KRISHNA
OM HARE OM — GOVINDA JAI GOPALA JAI
                            JAYA —

OM HARE OM — RADHA KRISHNA
OM HARE OM — RAMA RADHA
OM HARE OM — BALA SIVA
OM HARE OM — RAMA SITA.

REPEAT UNTIL DEATH.

George's handwritten lyrics for 'Gopala Krishna'
Right, George, Friar Park, 1970

Pages 242–43, George at an outdoor performance, Benares, India, 1974, from George's camera

I always felt that in spite of all the fame, all the hullabaloo around that time and all the time for years following, George had something which we call in our language *tyagi*, which means the feeling of unattachment. He had everything – all the wealth, all the fame, whatever he wanted. But he was not attached to it. It didn't seem to matter much to him, because he was searching for something much higher, much deeper. It does seem like he already had some Indian background in him. Otherwise, it's hard to explain how, from Liverpool, with his background, and then becoming so famous, what reason did he have to get so attracted to a particular type of life and philosophy, even religion? It seems very strange really. Unless you believe in reincarnation. RAVI SHANKAR

I think the best thing about Ravi is that, when you mention him being a classical musician people think he's this really boring, straight, intense musician, but he isn't. He's so funny, he's like a kid. Ever since I've known him, the accent has always been on enjoyment, on being happy, on having a laugh. He's the funniest person I've ever met. He's certainly not naïve. Just to be able to be his friend is an honour and a joy. The simplicity of the childlike tendency that's within him, it's very catchy. And that's why, I think, everybody who's met him or spent time with him just loves him. GEORGE

Above, George with Sripad Maharaj, Benares, India, 1974, from George's camera
Right, George and Ravi Shankar with Sripad Maharaj, Benares, India, 1974, from George's camera
Pages 248–49, Ravi Shankar, Benares, India, 1974, photograph by George

George on his thirtieth birthday, Friar Park, 1973, from George's camera

Pages 252–53, Murals at the Lake Palace Hotel, Lake Pichola, Udaipur, India, 1974, photograph by George

254   *Above and Right*, Lake Palace, Udaipur, India, 1974, from George's camera

George on Lake Pichola, Udaipur, India, 1974, from George's camera

Right, Murals at the Lake Palace, Udaipur, India, 1974, photograph by George

George called me and said, 'I'm going to India in January. Do you want to come along with me?' and I went, 'Yeah!' George and I stayed in this family's private home in Calcutta, a family who were very good friends of Ravi Shankar's, and every night we were treated to a fantastic meal and we'd go to these sites, especially the Kali temple that was a big spiritual place in Calcutta dedicated to the mother aspect of God, Kali. It was so amazing. There was so much to feast your eyes on.

We then went to Varanasi for the second part of the trip, because Ravi Shankar had a house there. Varanasi is the spiritual capital of India for the Hindus, because the Ganges goes through there and it's supposed to be a very auspicious and holy place.

I saw Ravi with his students, playing with them and teaching them ragas, and it was a wonderful experience seeing George interact with that whole thing. And we took a boat ride down the Ganges, passing the ghats where the cremations were occurring; in India they say that it's very holy for your body to end up in Benares and your ashes dumped into the Ganges. George always told me that he wanted his ashes to be put in the Ganges. He loved India.
GARY WRIGHT, *Musician and friend*

Gary Wright during trip to India with George, 1974
Right, George, India, 1974

George with Lakshmi Shankar, India, 1974
Right, George, India, 1976
Pages 262–63, George and Kumar Shankar, the Ganges, Benares, India, 1974

5

All
Things
Must
Pass

Now the darkness only stays at night time
In the morning it will fade away
Daylight is good at arriving at the right time
No it's not always going to be this grey
All things must pass

ALL THINGS PASS.

① Sunrise doesn't Last all Morning —
a Cloudburst doesn't last all Day —
Seems my Love is up, and has left you
with No Warning — But its not always
going to be this Grey —
All Things must Pass — All Things must Pass Away

② Sunset doesn't last all evening,
A Mind can blow those clouds away
After all this my love is up and must be
Leaving — but its not always going to be
this Grey, and all things must pass —
All things must pass Away —

BRIDGE   All things must Pass — None of Life's
Strings can Last — So — I must be on my
way... and face another Day —

③ Now Darkness only stays a night-time —
in the Morning it will fade away.
Daylight is Good at Arriving at the Right Time
       No its not always going to be this
Grey — all things must Pass All Things must Pass
       [REPEAT]   away.

George's handwritten lyrics for 'All Things Must Pass'

266   *Right*, George, Friar Park, 1970

Friar Park is like a Victorian gothic revival, mixed with a French chateau. It's really incredible. It was all rotting and nobody was interested. They were trying to pull it down and destroy it. Now it's a listed building. They even sent me certificates of historic value for the railings and restorations which I installed! All the historic societies want to come and look at it now, but nobody was interested in it when I got it, it was just unloved. I wrote a song about the fella who built it on *All Things Must Pass*, 'The Ballad of Sir Frankie Crisp'. GEORGE

When we came down we saw it and we went, 'My God! What's he done?' You know, look at it! People had dumped cars in the garden and brambles had grown over them. You didn't go for a walk without a machete in your hand to cut your way through. And it was a huge, huge project. There was grass growing up through some of the wooden floors. All the beautiful tracery work, a lot of that needed replacing. And the grounds, there was so much that was hidden. But somehow or other he had the foresight to look at it for what it was — and do it. IRENE HARRISON

George in the room that was to become his studio, Friar Park, 1970, from George's camera

Right, George's list of work to be done at Friar Park, 1970

Leaded lights missing from window to corridor
on 2ND floor near tower end at Back ✳
lead on Roof of rooms to be demolished for area
possibly outside room ▬▬▬▬ stayed in.
skylight on ▬▬▬ Toilet outside made Bigger
drain hole down, from checkered Balcony - to high
to take water? ▬▬ Lids fixing on open Tops of
drain pipes.
Drain pipes missing on ledge outside of 2ND floor
south side (▬▬▬▬▬▬ above main Bathroom
Big pipe missing off roof above turret room over
main suite
Clean out and fix holes to under Tower room
floor (exterior on roof). ✓

✳ Lead Roses missing from drain pipe outside this
window.
remove all old wires and radio ariels. ✓

From Roof) Main House)
Tower over 2ND floor Toilet ~~unblock~~ uncover
wooden design Between 2 tile levels.
Two Dormer window sides uncover - zinc
plates. (Bath + Toilet Rooms 2ND floor North Wing.
check out drain pipe ~~around~~ the Tower.
Repair all woodwork on windows and doors   + waterproof
to Roof spaces (Bolts missing).
Replace all missing Tiles and repair all Tiles
Repair and Paint all roof skylights plate glass

Tiles on vertical roof near shaft hanging out

Bell Tower interior + Exterior (woodwork)
            Clean Polish Bell etc ✓

windows onto roof repairing (new locks etc
window on side of flag pole - exit made
easier (more like a door). ✓

Replace lightning conductors? ✓

fit mesh onto drain pipe openings in Roof -

The Lodge, Friar Park.   Bignell, Bros., Woodcote, Reading.

There were trees there that were blue firs, and he said at the time, pointing them out, 'Do you realise that when Frank Crisp planted those he knew he was never ever going to see them? He planted those as a stand of trees. They must have gone in as saplings. So he knew that by the time he was an old gentleman he still wasn't going to see this garden looking as he'd planned it.' And he said, 'That's a huge task to take on. To try and look at something and think, I might never see this in my lifetime.' And I think that's how George looked at the park. That whatever he did or planned, he might never see it to its fruition, but whatever he did, he did well. IRENE HARRISON

Vintage postcard showing the grounds of Friar Park

Right, George in the rockery, Friar Park, 1971

272   George in the neglected grounds of Friar Park, 1970

George in the rockery, Friar Park, 1970   275

Let it Roll:
(Ballad of ~~Sir Frankie Crisp~~)

Let it Roll across the floor—thru the ~~Hall~~
and out ~~that in~~ the door—to ye fountain of Perpetual
Murth—Let it Roll for all ~~its~~ worth—(Let it Roll)

Find Me———— WHERE YE ECHO LAYS—
Lose yer bodies in the Maze.
~~Lepers squint~~——~~Abode of Francis Steed~~
See the Lord—and all the mouths He Feeds.
Let it Roll among the Weeds—

Let it Roll ~~down into~~ the Caves—
Ye long walks of Cool and Shade
through ye Woods—(~~HERE MAY YOU REST AWHILE~~)
——————— match your style.

Fools Illusions Everywhere—Jan & Moll ~~sweep~~
the Stairs—
Eyes that ~~shining~~ full of Inner Light
Let it Roll into the Night—

(oh Sir Frankie Crisp—etc).

George's handwritten lyrics for 'The Ballad of Sir Frankie Crisp (Let It Roll)'
Right, George in a grotto at Friar Park, 1970
Pages 278–79, Stained glass, 1970
276

'My Sweet Lord' has got a mantra in there and mantras are – well, they call it a mystical sound vibration encased in the syllable. The vibratory power in a mantra is released when it's repeated over and over. The word mantra has been used up a bit by people, newspapers and stuff. Like they wrecked the word guru, they turned it into anything. Guru means the dispeller of darkness. So, the word mantra, now they use it for anything. 'The prime minister's mantra is "Give us your money"'– things like that. Anyway it has this power within it and it's just hypnotic, and it's kind of nice. Once I chanted it for like three days non-stop, driving through Europe, and you just get hypnotised, you get on some subtle level, which makes you feel so good that you don't want to stop. GEORGE

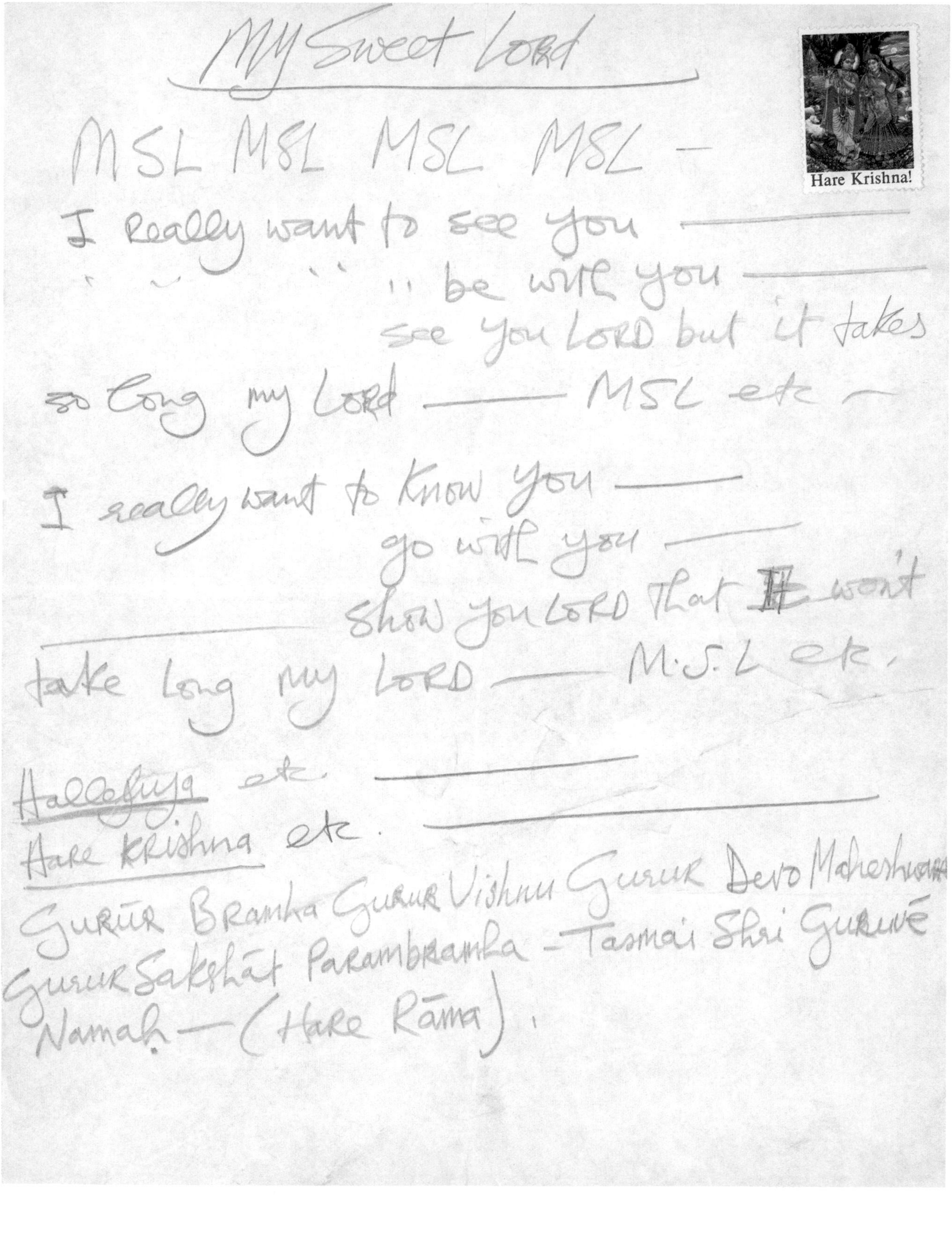

My Sweet Lord

MSL MSL MSL MSL —
I really want to see you ————
"   "   " be with you ————
    see you LORD but it takes
so long my Lord ———— MSL etc —

I really want to know you ————
    go with you ————
———— show you LORD that it won't
take long my LORD ———— M.S.L etc.

Halleluja etc. ————————
Hare Krishna etc. ——————————
Gurur Bramha Gurur Vishnu Gurur Devo Maheshwara
Gurur Sakshat Parambramha — Tasmai Shri Gurve
Namah — (Hare Rama).

I went to George's Friar Park, which he had just purchased, and he said, 'I have a few ditties for you to hear.' It was endless! He had literally hundreds of songs, and each one was better than the rest. He had all this emotion built up when it was released to me. I don't think he had played them to anybody, maybe Pattie.

He let me make all the basic tracks. He said, 'Go, go, go!' He would play and then he would come back in and listen. In the overdubbing, he was in control of his parts. He wouldn't let anything go until it was right. 'My Sweet Lord' must have taken about twelve hours to overdub the guitar solos. He must have had that in triplicate, six-part harmony, before we decided on two-part harmony. Perfectionist is not the word. Anyone can be a perfectionist. He was beyond that. He just had to have it so right. He would try and try and experiment upon experiment, to the point where I would leave the studio for several hours while he played different parts over and over with the engineer. Then I would come in and listen, and he would say, 'How does it sound? Are there too many parts? Too few parts?' He'd do the same thing with the background vocals. He was a great harmoniser with himself – he could do all the parts by himself.

He could play like nobody else because he had his own style of playing. I don't think George would say he was as meticulous and fluent as Eric. He always bowed to Eric as far as a technician. But for versatility and ideas, George was far superior. George was more creative, more melodic. Eric was a better player, more blues-oriented, and George asked Eric to play a lot of the solos on the *All Things Must Pass* album and sit in the control room with me while Eric played them. But on the commercial recordings like 'My Sweet Lord', George played those, and worked on them for endless hours getting the harmonies right, because that's what made The Beatles' records, those solos. They were so commercial and so technically perfect. That was George's gift. George was one of the most commercial musicians and songwriters and quintessential players I've ever known in my entire career. PHIL SPECTOR, *Producer*

284   *Above and Right*, George and Phil Spector producing *The Concert for Bangladesh*, 1971

This war was going on between Pakistan and East Pakistan, as it was then known, which was part of the original whole of Bengal – that's where I belong to. All my distant relatives along with many other refugees there were coming by thousands through Calcutta, and all the women and children were suffering, and that made me feel very concerned. I was thinking of giving a performance, maybe with a few other Indian musicians who were around, and try to raise thirty to fifty thousand dollars, maybe. I thought that might help a little to send money to these refugee camps. George happened to be there in Los Angeles at that time and he saw how concerned and unhappy I was. I told him everything and he immediately felt that he would help in this, and I was overjoyed by that. It happened so quickly; within a few weeks he phoned all his friends, Bob Dylan, Eric Clapton and Billy Preston and many others, and fixed Madison Square Garden. It was really a miracle. RAVI SHANKAR

Ravi came to me and he said that if he was to do a concert he'd maybe play to so many thousand people. But with the size of the problem, the funds that would be made would just be so small. So that's why I came along. I can generate money by doing concerts and by making records. All I am trying to do is generate enough money and make sure the money is distributed in order to relieve some of the agony. GEORGE

There were two concerts: one in the afternoon at two, and one at eight o'clock. And it was magical. That's the only word to describe it, because nobody had ever seen anything like that before, that amount of star power onstage, since Woodstock, and this was all in two hours onstage at one time. It was chaos – we only had three hours to mic the band, then the audience came in, and we didn't know how to mic the audience. So the two concerts took four hours. The mixing took six months. And we had to put together what was a Grammy-winning album. PHIL SPECTOR

In one day, the whole world knew the name of Bangladesh. It was a fantastic occasion, and I think it was the first of its kind. Now, of course, wonderful things are done, so many musicians are raising money for different causes. But the Bangladesh concert, I think, was the very first one. RAVI SHANKAR

286   Ravi Shankar and George during the Concert for Bangladesh, 1971

George's notes for the Concert for Bangladesh, and pencil sketch of sleeve designs for Ravi Shankar's single 'Joi Bangla / Oh Bhagawan' (released on Apple Records), 1971

ॐ

Bangla Desh

~~Bangala Desh~~.

INTRO
When my friend came to me
With Sadness in his eyes
And told me that he wanted help
To try to save some live's   [Before a country die's]

Although I couldn't feel the pain
I knew I had to try
And so I'm asking all of you-to let me tell you Why.

① Bangala Dhiesh - Bangala Dēsh
Where so many people are dying fast
and it sure looks like a mess
I've never seen such distress
Now wont you lend your hand-please try to understand
~~Bangla-City~~ relieve the people of Bangla Dēsh

② Bangala-Dēsh, Bangala Dēsh
Such a great disaster - I dont understand
but it sure looks like a mess
I've never known such distress
Now please dont turn away-I want to hear you say
relieve the people of Bangala-Dēsh
<u>Solo</u>

③ Bangala-Desh, Bangala-Desh
Now it may seem so far, from where we all are
it's something we cant reject
This suffering I cant neglect
Now wont you give some bread
to get the starving fed, we got to relieve
Bangala-Desh.

George and Leon Russell backstage at the Concert for Bangladesh, New York, 1971

Right, George with Klaus Voormann, Jim Horn and the band during rehearsals for the Concert for Bangladesh, New York, 1971

George performing at the Concert for Bangladesh, New York, 1971

Right, George and Bob Dylan performing at the Concert for Bangladesh, New York, 1971

Apple

Sept. 1, 1971

Mr. James Keltner
3006 Maxwell Street
Hollywood, California 90027

Dear Jim:

VENDOR NUMBER	INVOICE NUMBER	INVOICE DATE	M.S.G. VOUCHER NO.	GROSS AMOUNT	DISCOUNT	NET AMOUNT
	ck.req.	8/12/71	H-200038	$ 243,418.50		$ 243,418.50

In payment of Box Office Receipts for the George Harrison & Friends
Concert held at Madison Square Garden - August 1, 1971

IF INCORRECT RETURN WITH EXPLANATION DETACH BEFORE DEPOSITING
fm
NET TOTAL $ 243,418.50

MADISON SQUARE GARDEN CENTER, INC.
FOUR PENNSYLVANIA PLAZA/NEW YORK, N.Y. 10001
1-12
210 26

NOT VALID AFTER 30 DAYS
CHECK NUMBER
A 4476

Chemical Bank
TWO PENNSYLVANIA PLAZA
(7TH AVENUE AT 33RD STREET)
NEW YORK, N.Y.

EXACTLY $$243418 AND 50 CTS

PAY TO THE ORDER OF
DATE 8/12/71 $ 243,418.50

UNITED NATIONS CHILDREN'S FUND
FOR RELIEF TO REFUGEE CHILDREN OF
BANGLA DESH

Thank you for all your help.

Hare Kṛṣṇa

George Harrison

Letter from George to Jim Keltner, thanking him for his participation in the Concert for Bangladesh, September, 1971
Right, Letter from Ravi Shankar to George thanking him for staging the Concert for Bangladesh, August, 1971

HOTEL **Navarro**
ON-THE-PARK
112 central park south, new york, n.y. 10019
212 circle 7-7900
Cable NAVARROTEL

Dear Dear George,

My deep gratitude
to you for doing what you did! A
great cause, & a great achievment!
It also gave you the confidence
and strength of what great things
You can do _____ unlimited things
- ~~for~~ not for yourself only but
many others! Please start a personal
~~Campgian~~ (spelling wrong!) ~ to help
Campaign

the kids to keep away foom the
Drugs! I know it has to be done
with love & feeling to convince them
and not to make it worse by
antigonizing them. Which is only possible
when you win their love & respect!

Swami Vishnu in yoga peacock pose shows man should be free as a bird.

The Peace Plane painted by Peter Max for Swami Vishnu's world boundary breaking tour

Just how United are the Nations? For the forest to be green each tree must be green. It's like saying all the different nations have their own cultures, they all have their own backgrounds, they all have their own problems, so you have a lot of trouble in the world. But after all, there are a lot of different trees and a lot of different flowers in a garden but they're all made out of sap. There must be something that underlies all nations, all cultures, all colours, all races, all religions. There's one underlying truth which relates to them all. And that's it, for the forest to be green every tree must be green.

यदा यदा हि धर्मस्य ग्लानिर्भवति भारत ।
अभ्युत्थानमधर्मस्य तदात्मानं सृजाम्यहम् ॥ ७ ॥

Whenever there is decline of
righteousness, O Arjuna, and rise of
unrighteousness, then I manifest Myself.

GITA IV-7
(LORD KRISHNA)

परित्राणाय साधूनां विनाशाय च दुष्कृताम् ।
धर्मसंस्थापनार्थाय संभवामि युगे युगे ॥ ८ ॥

For the protection of the good, for the
destruction of the wicked and for the
establishment of righteousness,
I am born in every age.

GITA IV-7
(LORD KRISHNA)

Bearer must sign on photo   A signer par le titulaire

NAME
NOM   GEORGE HARRISON

Bearer was randomly born on earth in :   LIVERPOOL
Le titulaire est né accidentellement sur terre à :

Country of :
Pays :   ENGLAND.

Date de naissance / Date of birth **25·2·43**	Taille / Height **5·10½**	
Poids / Weight **136 lbs**	Cheveux / Hair **BROWN**	Yeux / Eyes **BROWN**

Present address :   Rue Street   FRIAR PARK

Adresse actuelle :   Ville City HENLEY on THAMES   Etat State OXON·ENGLAND

Issued by the True World Order (TWO.)
Emis par l'Ordre de la Fraternité Mondial
Sivananda Ashram — Camp de Yoga
8th Avenue, Val Morin, Quebec, Canada   Swami Vishnudevananda

Signed   Swami Vishnudevananda

Fondateur-président   **Swami Vishnu-devananda**   Founder-president

Just for all of us standing here now, none of us can relate to each other unless we can relate to ourselves, we must find ourselves really. Each country must be strong and united. As soon as we can all have Planet Earth passports I'll be grateful, because I'm tired of being British or being white, or being a Christian or a Hindu. I don't have a philosophy, I just believe in the sap that runs throughout.   GEORGE, UNICEF press conference, New York, 1974

Dark Horse Tour band: from left to right (back row): Chuck Findley
(trumpet), Tom Scott (saxophone), Willie Weeks (bass guitar),
Andy Newmark (drums), Billy Preston (keyboards), Alla Rakha
(tabla), Ravi Shankar (sitar), George, Satyadev Pawar (North India
violin), Harihar Rao (percussion), Robben Ford (guitar), (front row)
L. Subramaniam (South India violin), Kamalesh Maitra (percussion),
T. V. Gopalkrishnan (mridangam and vocal), Hariprasad Chaurasia
(flute), Viji Shankar (vocal), Shivkumar Sharma (santoor), Lakshmi
Shankar (vocal), Gopal Krishan (vichitra veena), Kartick Kumar (sitar),
Emil Richards (percussion), Sultan Khan (sarangi) and Rijram Desad

(percussion and strings), Los Angeles, 1974, from George's camera

Ravi Shankar directing the recording
sessions for *Shankar Family and Friends*
with musicians including Klaus Voormann,
Harihar Rao, Kumar Shankar, Emil Richards,
George and Ray Kramer, Los Angeles, 1973   301

After I got into Indian music I went back to India and recorded some music in HMV in Bombay, and downstairs in the basement they had this incredible stock of records, and the fellow let me go through and take whatever records I wanted. So I stocked up on everything that looked interesting. I took maybe one hundred records, and I got into every type of Indian classical music, but it was always solo, or the most you got was a *jugalbandi*, a duet, two people playing together. But 'Nava Rasa Ranga' was this amazing piece of Ravi's. I don't know how many singers he actually had because I only ever heard it on tape, but there was a big group singing. I listened to it so many times and for years I kept saying, 'Let's do "Nava Rasa Ranga".' I set up the Material World Charitable Foundation and I got some money into it by donating some of my song publishing, and then I went to India in January 1974 and got Ravi to organise not exactly 'Nava Rasa Ranga' but something very similar to that. It was called the Music Festival from India and we came to Ravi's house in Benares and arranged a tour.

First, Ravi brought all these musicians and they came to Henley-on-Thames. Ravi stayed in London. All the other musicians stayed at the Imperial Hotel in Henley. I had this big car that John and Yoko had bought, and then they left England so I took it – it was a stretch 600 Mercedes, a white one with blacked-out windows, and it would pull up outside Friar Park and the doors would open and Alla Rakha and all of them would get out! It was great.

Ravi would come up from London and be making up the music on the way. It was amazing, because he'd sit there and say to one person, 'This is where you play,' and the next one, 'And you do this,' and 'You do that,' and they're all going, What? 'OK, one, two, three…' and you'd think, 'This is going to be a catastrophe' – and it would be the most amazing thing.

I always remember what Maharishi said consciousness was supposed to be: the maximum effect in the shortest time with the least expenditure of energy. Musically, Ravi could do that with maybe four instruments and make it sound like an orchestra. I don't know the secret, but it certainly works. GEORGE

Ravi Shankar directing the recording sessions for *Shankar Family and Friends,* Los Angeles, 1973

Ravi Shankar directing musicians in rehearsals for Music Festival from India (performed at the Royal Albert Hall and on a brief European tour), 1974

Pages 306-7, Music Festival from India musicians (back row from left): Harihar Rao, Rijram Desad, Hariprasad Chaurasia, Viji Shankar, Lakshmi Shankar, Sultan Khan, Kumar Shankar, Kamalesh Maitra, (middle row from left) Kartick Kumar, Shivkumar Sharma, Alla Rakha, T. V. Gopalkrishnan, L. Subramaniam, (front row) George, Billy the cat and Ravi Shankar, 1974

308   Billboard on Sunset Strip, Los Angeles, 1973

I think over the years Ravi's come to see what gets various audiences excited in the West. We experienced this when we did the tour in 1974 with the Indian musicians, and the rock audience that was watching him. Whatever they said in the papers, the audience always gave a standing ovation to the drummers. You put one of those drummers on, let him play a solo and people were just falling over, they couldn't believe it. And that's been the thing in Ravi's classical concerts: just as Zakir Hussain says, he allowed space and freedom for the accompanists which never existed before that. They weren't given the spotlight on their own, but he allowed that. It was also a smart move because realising how fantastic the tabla is, just the sound of it, those rhythms featuring in his concert meant that the audience would get really excited. GEORGE

KODAK TRI-X PAN FILM
KODAK SAF.ETY FILM
KODAK TRI-X
KODAK SAF.ETY FILM
6 3 0 9 0

I was not in a perfect condition to be doing that tour. I was really wiped out. That year I'd flown to India, arranged for all the Indian musicians to come over, came back and produced an album by Splinter, two guys from Tyneside. I'd produced the album with Ravi and all his musicians, and organised this concert tour, and at the same time I was trying to make my own album. So I was knackered by the time I got to Los Angeles for the rehearsal, and I was still trying to finish my album at the time. Then suddenly, singing ten hours a day in rehearsal, I lost my voice. I had the choice then to decide whether I would cancel the tour or go and sing like Louis Armstrong!

In spite of that, the audiences I thought were fantastic, they always gave a standing ovation for the Indian musicians. But I think it was a bit ahead of the general public. We had about sixteen Indian musicians and about ten western musicians. I played one part with the westerns, then we played a part all together, and then the Indians played a section, and then we finished up. I'm not saying that all the audiences didn't understand it because I know a lot of people did enjoy that concert. I think it was just too much at that time, the combination of everything. But I enjoyed it.   GEORGE

George on stage at Madison Square Garden, New York City, Dark Horse Tour, 1974

Page 314-15, George and Olivia waiting for the band to clear Customs in Vancouver, Dark Horse Tour, 1974

The critics were brutal about Ravi opening the show, and about George's voice being gone. But that's the way it is with critics, they have to be critical. That did not deter George. And by the way, not everybody was bored with it, and not everybody thought that his voice sounded horrible. They just loved hearing those songs and him trying to deliver them the best he could. There's a soulfulness about that, and there's a courage about that, and I think most of his fans saw and felt that.

I've seen what it's like on other tours when they don't love you. From my perspective, George, on the '74 tour, he was loved. JIM KELTNER, *Musician*

George on stage at the Capital Center, Landover, Maryland, Dark Horse Tour, 1974

6

Handled
with
Care

'Scan not a friend with a microscopic glass. You know his faults, now let his foibles pass.' That helped me actively to ease up on whosoever I thought I loved. It gave me the consciousness not to hang onto the negative side of it, to be more forgiving.   GEORGE

Anything to do with racing and cars and motorbikes, that was part of George's world. Then there was the music side and then there was the movie side, then there was the comedian side, and it was always this wonderful crowd of people all pretending to be grown-ups. And that's what was really funny about it, and we all just giggled a lot, because, 'Look at this! And we're all in this place.'

I've always been intrigued with George's spirituality, which is absolutely essential to him. But he was living in the material world. So he was caught in these two worlds, a very spiritual world and a very material world. And they're related in the sense that it's about finding the beauty in the real world to create, to make the real world as beautiful as it can be. That's, I think, what he was doing in Friar Park. He created such exquisite beauty there, but there was nothing airy-fairy about it, and it wasn't about somebody snapping his fingers and having somebody else do it for him. He had to do the work. He chose where the stones went. He chose the trees and put them there. Handmade is what his world was. TERRY GILLIAM, *Python*

We could laugh at the world. We could undercut the seriousness of things all the time. Pomposity and authority and hypocrisy – these are things that we all agreed needed to be chopped off at the knees. The problem when you get to be as successful and famous as people like George is there's too many sycophants around you. It's really hard to hold them at bay, and he was very good at it, much better than most people that I've met who have been that successful. TERRY GILLIAM

Above and Right, George jamming with Spike Milligan (beloved English comedian of *The Goon Show*), 1973, from George's camera

We had written *The Life of Brian*. We had EMI putting up the money for the movie. We had designed it. We were heading out on a Saturday with the crew to Tunisia to start building, and on Thursday we get a call, and Lord Delfont – Bernie, to his friends – had finally got around to reading the script apparently. He hadn't read it before, and he was shocked and horrified and he said, 'There's no way EMI is going to be involved in this blasphemous filth.' And they pulled the plug on a Thursday, and we were dead. TERRY GILLIAM

We were looking for four million dollars. Nobody has that amount of money. But eventually when we finally got to California, George says, 'Yeah, I figured it out. We're going to create a company and we're going to give you the money, and it's four million dollars.' And he mortgaged his house to put up the money for this movie because he wanted to see it, which is still the most anybody's ever paid for a cinema ticket. It was the most extraordinary act of benevolence and farsightedness. He paid for the entire film. I think the reason he did it is because he was a Python fan. You could not get through the door without seventeen lines being quoted. I mean, on tour he called himself Jack Lumber. And it was a bit like Bialystock and Bloom, him and his manager, because they can't possibly have imagined it was going to make any money. And of course it did, it started to make money, which was like, Oh No! ERIC IDLE, *Python*

It was really a one-off. Basically I was just a Python fan. I asked my manager, 'Can you think of how to get them the money?' And he came back to me in a week and said, 'I think I know how we could do it. We'll be the producers.' So we mortgaged all our companies and everything, borrowed the money from the bank and did it. And fortunately, it made the money back at least. I think we actually made some money on that which then went in towards *Time Bandits*, which was the Python spin-off of Terry Gilliam's. So we originally started just as the one-off, but then I sort of rolled along with it. GEORGE

The phone rang. 'What are you doing?' said George. I said, 'Well, I'm not doing a lot.' And he said, 'Well, I think I've got a film company. Why don't you be me in the office?' It was as simple as that. RAY COOPER, *Musician, Head of Development and Production at HandMade Films*

With *Time Bandits*, he wrote the song that goes over the end credits and it was very late in the day that I realised what he was saying in the song, because it turned out to be his notes for me about what he liked and didn't like about the film. It's all in the lyrics. And everything is about how it goes on too long – he didn't phrase it like that – you know, you're here to amaze then get out quickly before you bore us to tears. And there's also comment about me being arrogant and not listening! And I thought it was the most brilliant, subtle, clever thing a man could ever do, to write a song. He's writing about things that he felt strongly about and yet he's too polite and decent and, I think, respectful of other artists, whatever form that takes, to interfere.
TERRY GILLIAM

SONG FOR SWINGING TIME BANDITS BY GEORGE.

① OH RY IN EYE AY — OH RY IN EYE AY
OH RY IN EYE KEY OOH LAY
KA LAY OOH LAU-EE — OH RY IN EY AY
SYA TE LEE AY VEE SHOW.

Re Wr 1

Hail, Rain, Sleet, Wind, Lightening, Thunder
~~I See Ice and Snow~~ (and the) TIME BANDITS ~~they all know~~
Skies as Black as ~~(DAY)~~ — ~~only a dream~~ ~~(AWAY)~~ A~~go~~

② OH RY ETC... ~~Snow only a dream Ago.~~
ROB, THIEVE, CHEAT, STEAL, Loot and Plunder CRAZILY they
FALL ~~Escape through~~ Space and TIME ~~TIME BANDITS on the Go.~~
~~GONE WITHOUT DELAY~~ -only a dream A~~go~~.

MIDDLE ~~~~ AWAY ~~PAST~~
 * Tumbleing ~~through~~ the 13th Century
You Wont get half ~~the~~ Chance to catch a Rest in
MYTHOLOGY.
        The Treasures of History: to be found
        Near the Legends of Time — All the Handiworks Remain,
there _____ only a Dream Away.

                                    + CO only A Dream Ago.
OH RY IN — ETC... ~~Evil ogres — century away~~
③ Supreme Being here with Evil Genius, ~~an C~~ ~~Play~~ WE
the Time Bandits say 'Hello'.. WE ARE STAY —
Evil ogres — Supreme Beings ~~~~ the Play
④ OH RY ETC.... ~~Altogether~~ only a Dream Away
                                    ~~PLAY.~~
Wally, Randall, Strutter, Vermin — Og and fidget ~~too~~
~~Time BANDITS Motley Crew.~~ (after you) STRAY
        SHARING THEIR DREAM with You
All together Now.   (A)   only A ~~Dreaming~~ Away
        OH RY IN EY AY ETC..... .

                (* tumble Away past the 13th Century.

George and Dhani on the set of *Time Bandits* with Terry Gilliam, David Warner, John Cleese, Mike Edmonds, Tiny Ross, Jack Purvis, David Rappaport, Malcolm Dixon and Kenny Baker, 1981

HandMade was called HandMade because we were handmade. Everything was done in-house, including quite a lot of the marketing strategy. We designed posters, because we had people like Terry Gilliam who would do those designs. And we had people like Michael Palin and Derek Taylor who would come up with great bylines. This was all in-house. So again this was like a giant band and George loved being in a band, and this is why the Wilburys came about. He missed working with people. He was a great collaborator.

I was a great believer, and George believed in this too, that we were in a world that was too highly specialised, and if you were a musician who understood timing, understood how to listen, how to have a voice when you're a solo instrument, how to be an accompanist, it wasn't too big a bridge to build to developing a good story or to understanding the egos of actors or directors. So one could move into these areas fairly seamlessly if you had humility. RAY COOPER

We tend to do films which other companies don't do because they're not really that commercial. Yet I think that if something's really good it deserves to be made. And as long as we can make it within a limited budget and we can get it put out and hopefully recoup that money, we're not into the idea of making millions. It would be wonderful if suddenly *Withnail and I* made a hundred million dollars, but it's not going to. But as long as there's an audience out there of people who do actually like films that you have to use your intelligence for. The same with *Mona Lisa*. These films go out in a sort of a more humble way, a smaller distribution, but there's an audience for them and those films also build. GEORGE

George with Ray Cooper and Richard E. Grant on the set of *How to Get Ahead in Advertising*, 1989
Right, George and Ray Cooper in front of the Mark Boyle work *Holland Park Avenue Study*, 1967 as used on the cover of *Somewhere in England*,
Tate Gallery, London, 1981

The first five years of HandMade Films were celebrated with success after success and I found myself having the great privilege of working with wonderful artists/filmmakers which was also a huge and joyous learning curve.

I think George hated industry as a concept, but what he loved was collaboration. He had a voice of reason and consideration in filmmaking and he felt part of that community, rather than the film industry. I think he was a bit embarrassed by being the owner of a film company in that sense. He was very proud of it, but the idea of being a part of that industry, and with all that that meant – Hollywood, the turmoil, and the arguments and the fights over cuts – George didn't want to be involved in that side of it.

We suffered our disappointments, but that was almost inevitable. We were a young, passionate company after all! But HandMade stood out as a leader and an innovator. We started to help shape a new, independent British film style and identity, and HandMade was firmly at the helm of this magical period. Films like *The Life of Brian*, *Time Bandits*, *The Long Good Friday*, *Withnail and I*, *Mona Lisa*, *A Private Function* and so many more helped shape a new age and genre of British film, and these were films that probably would never have been made by any other company in the industry. That was the strength of George's belief in his friends and fellow artists. It was also inevitable that in this process new careers would be forged, new talent would blossom. Terry Gilliam, Bob Hoskins, Bruce Robinson, Michael Palin, Neil Jordan, Richard E. Grant, Richard Griffiths and many more reciprocated George's belief and embrace. In the early days that was how George wanted HandMade to be, a wonderful collaborative playground where his friends and colleagues could bring their passions for film together and good work could be and was achieved.

Perhaps this was the real 'United Artists', but 'HandMade' was a much more interesting name. RAY COOPER

George was always called 'the Quiet One', and I always thought that was a terrible misnomer because whenever I was with him he never stopped – he'd talk about anything, and he had very strong opinions on lots of things, always wanting to learn something else. MICHAEL PALIN

George with Michael Palin on the set of *The Missionary*, 1982

I was twelve when I saw Liverpool's first British Grand Prix, in Aintree, and saw Fangio and Stirling Moss for Mercedes-Benz. I followed Formula One until the time we started being professional musicians, and even then in the Sixties, though we were so busy, I caught a few races, mainly Monte Carlo. Then I met Jackie Stewart and it was really through him that I got backstage, and it's much more interesting back there. Jackie was the outspoken world champion, and he was one of the greatest, if not the greatest. Three-times world champion, and he lived to tell the story. My song 'Faster' is largely to do with Jackie. In fact I lifted the title from his book.

It's fascinating when you can know the drivers and the teams and all their problems, and you can see them as people. Because they are just people, but to go to work they have to get in this car and do 180 miles an hour. GEORGE

When you're driving a racing car to the absolute limit of its ability, and that of your own ability, it's a very unique emotion and experience, but it's a unique unity of man and machine, to take it to both limits. When that happens, your senses are so magnified for feel, for motion. You're going to the absolute limit of the car's tyres and suspension, the aerodynamics, and you yourself are right at the very edge of your limit. When that happens, your senses are so strong.

That's what I think George saw in racing. We talked about things like that a lot: heightened senses, of your feel and your touch, and your feet – because of the pedals, the gas pedals, the brake pedals, the sensitivity of the function of those – and your own hands on the steering wheel. You don't grab a steering wheel. A steering wheel should be caressed. You're more sensitive when you're not grabbing things. Caressing the car into doing the things that you want it to do, sometimes against its own will, that's the kind of thing George and I talked about it, and he would love that. If you listen to a really top guitarist, or any top musician, and how they can make that guitar talk, or that keyboard talk, or the skins talk, that's another heightening of senses that is beyond the ken, the knowledge of any normal man or woman. I think that is where I got my buzz out of motor racing. Not the element of danger, certainly not from fear, but from the senses that were so high and so stimulating, so fulfilling. You get driven by it. I think the really good musicians must be doing the same thing. The only difference was that in our case, we were so close to death. JACKIE STEWART, *Formula One World Champion*

George with Formula One world champions Emerson Fittipaldi and Jackie Stewart, Brazilian Grand Prix, São Paulo, 1979

Looking back on it now I am kind of horrified that I had the nerve to do it, but I was in my early twenties and desperate to become a racing driver, and I knew that George liked motor racing, so I wrote to him to see if he could help. And he was interested. 'Look, I want to help,' he said, 'because I really liked your dad.' So from that point onwards I had a Beatle sponsor in the background. I really was shocked that he actually said that he would help. But he helped lots of people in different ways that you never get to hear about, so I didn't like to talk about it. I felt really grateful to George for helping me out at a time when I really needed a leg up.

I've been in his car, his McLaren F1, and anyone who likes to drive a fast car like that is interested in this idea of being taken on a journey, going out of this world in a small way and experiencing something which is mind-blowing, because it is quite mind-blowing driving a Formula One car. But I said to George once, 'I really would love to go on a rocket. That's my biggest dream, to go on a rocket and go into space.' And he said, 'No, man. Inner space, not outer space.' So he would also sort of bring me back down to earth, I suppose.

He was intrigued by why people would want to risk their lives doing it. But he was also excited. He liked the competition. This is where there's a contradiction, because he actually could get quite animated about the opposition. He was a fighter. DAMON HILL, *Formula One World Champion*

The very top racing drivers have the ability to go to a higher level of thought, where they process the information much quicker, which is really slowing stuff down. The inputs that you need to drive a racing car are your ears, your eyes, your bottom, your ribs, your hands and your feet. That's where you get the feeling from, for the G-forces, and for when the car's going to let go. The people that can slow all that down and process all those inputs in a way where they can get through a particular corner more quickly and more precisely than somebody else, those are the really good guys. And I suspect that's very similar to somebody doing meditation, because I imagine that's what you do. You slow everything down so you take the inputs and multiply them.

I think it might've been a side attraction of racing that George could draw a parallel between meditation, that form of mind control, and what racing drivers have to do to drive quickly. There might have been a connection there. But I don't think it was the main attraction. GORDON MURRAY, *Formula One and McLaren F1 designer*

After George had commissioned the F1, he counted down the weeks. Each car took three months to build. They were truly handmade. He almost drove us mad while we were building the car: 'Could you fit just another elephant in?' But it was good fun. As it got nearer the time for the collection, he could hardly wait. He loved the car, not just because it was something he'd seen from its conception right through to having his own personalised car; he loved it as a sports car as well. It is a pretty frightening experience to drive one: 630 horsepower with no ABS, no power brakes, no power steering, no traction control. He loved that. And he loved the noise it made as well. GORDON MURRAY

· HAND BUILT FOR GEORGE HARRISON · DECEMBER 1994

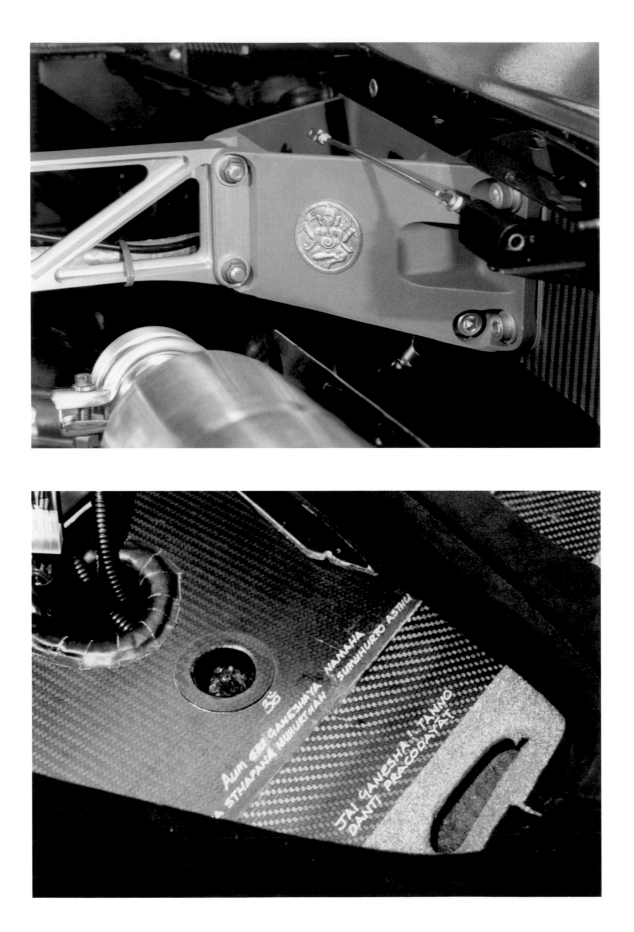

I was a bit tired of making records by about 1981, thought I'd have a rest, but I kept writing those years I didn't make an album. When I felt it was a good time to make a record, the one thing was to have a producer, because on my previous records I'd worked all alone. Got a bit bogged down, I felt. I needed a bit of input. So that's when I figured out Jeff Lynne would be good. So I went out and hunted him down, and tricked him into producing *Cloud Nine* with me. I'd been a fan of his, and also we're similar, inasmuch as he's a songwriter, guitar player and singer. GEORGE

George asked me, 'Would you like to go on holiday so we can get to know each other before we get in the studio? So that if the going gets a bit rough then we'll know how to deal with it.' So we went on holiday. We went to watch the Grand Prix in Adelaide. I had never been to Formula One before and it was just magnificent. Of course he knew all the drivers, and he knew all the teams, and that was my first taste of hanging out with George and a whole new life. It went on from there like that, all great things. We came back the best of friends and we remained that. JEFF LYNNE, *Musician and producer*

Normally I don't write with other people, but we worked on three songs together and it was quite interesting, because normally the way I work is I write the song, the melody and the lyrics, have it more or less completed – maybe occasionally I've got one or two lyrics that need finishing – but it's more or less completed before I put the track down. With Jeff, we tend to figure out the tune and the chords but have no idea how the melody or the lyrics are going to be and just see what happens that way. That was quite interesting: we had completed backing tracks with no melody and no lyrics. I said, 'Well I've got a few ideas, what are you thinking of?' He said, 'Oh, there's about three tunes. This could go about three different ways.' You leave your options open till the final vocal session. GEORGE

George with ukulele, Friar Park, 1979

He came in with two ukuleles and gave me one. 'You gotta play this thing, it's great! Let's jam.' I have no idea how to play a ukulele. 'Oh, it's no problem, I'll show you.' So we spent the rest of the day playing ukuleles, strolling around the yard. My wrist hurt the next day. But he taught me how to play it, and a lot of the chord formations. When he was going I walked out to the car and he said, 'Well, wait… I want to leave some ukuleles here.' He'd already given me one, so I said, 'Well, I've got this.' 'No, we may need more!' He opened his trunk and he had a lot of ukuleles in there, and I think he left four at my house. He said, 'Well, you never know when we might need them, because not everybody carries one around.' TOM PETTY

The first time I ever met George, we had just moved to Shiplake, outside of Henley, and we were up at Alvin Lee's house one night. We were all playing together and George came over to me afterwards and said, 'Now that's the kind of playing I like to hear. Tidy playing. If you want to impress me, that's the way to play.'

Another time he said, 'The thing about Ry Cooder is, if you soloed his guitar track, you wouldn't hear any other strings being played. He's so clean. That's what I'm trying to do.' With his kind of slide playing, George would mute the other strings so that they wouldn't ring when he was playing.

There was a little boy from India, U. Srinivas, that George played me a record of one day. This boy played on a little custom electric mandolin – he was only eleven or twelve at the time. He sounded like the Van Halen of India. Instead of doing his vibrato in a normal way, he would do it sideways; he would go across the frets and would make this kind of stuttering noise. It was a completely different way of playing. He was so fast, like lightning, and George was very impressed by this boy. I showed him one day: 'This is how he does it.' I played some Indian lines and I did the sideways vibrato. Then George started doing that later, I think on his last album. He was playing slide and doing that sideways thing.

I always think that he came up with things that other guitarists would never ever think of. He had a different way of looking at the guitar. He was like more of an artist of the guitar, in a way. GARY MOORE, *Musician*

George had such a beautiful touch on the slide. He had the kind of sound that would make you cry. In fact I do well up nowadays when I hear certain songs that he played slide on.

All the guitar players in the business know that George was incredible. Most of the regular folks don't think of him as a Clapton, and he wasn't, he didn't have those kind of chops, but what he had was so tremendous musically, so inventive, and so soulful, that he influenced a massive part of a generation of guitar players. JIM KELTNER

 George with Carl Perkins and Jeff Lynne in the studio, 1989

Carl is such a sweet fellow and obviously he influenced me a great deal when I was young. I was so into his music. Well, I still am. I just got all his old Sun Records originals on CD and they still sound great.

To jump on 'The Carl Perkins Show' with a good bunch of people, doing songs which we all know, is one thing. Or going on singing two or three tunes on The Prince's Trust with a good back-up band who know your tunes. But to do a tour is hard work. You've got to get your band, find out who's going to work for the band, rehearse and get all your sounds and lighting, and all the crew, and set up in the daytime. It's like when the army plans an invasion. GEORGE

The Traveling Wilburys recording, Los Angeles, 1987: (above left) Tom Petty and Bob Dylan, (below left) Roy Orbison, Jeff Lynne and George,

352 (above right) Roy Orbison, (below right) George and Tom Petty

B2

Maybe Somewhere down the Road Aways.
You'll think of me, wonder where I am these Days.
Maybe somewhere down the Road when somebody plays
PURPLE HAZE.

Well its alright, even if you're Peeling Apart.
As long as you still got a heart

B3

Dont Have to Be Ashamed of the Car I Drive.
Im Just Glad to Be Here, Happy to be Alive.
It dont Matter if you're by my Side.
IM SATISFIED

As Long as You're BRAIN Dont fade.
~~then you really got it made~~.
As long as you know ~~where if you're not in the gang~~
who you laid

6 even if they ~~things you~~ got bugged —
~~Just as long as you~~
As long as nobody get mugged.

Riding around in the Breeze
If you live the Life you Please ✓

its alright even if you happen to be white
even if you're all alone in the Night

Original lyrics to 'End of the Line' by the Traveling Wilburys

Right, Bob Dylan holding a sheet of Wilbury lyrics, Los Angeles, 1987

He and Jeff had kind of pictured this group, the Traveling Wilburys. George's idea was that he would handpick everybody in the band, and it'd be the perfect little band. But I think the qualifications were more about who you could hang out with than trying to find the best guy that did this or that. Though George liked to surround himself with people that were good at something. TOM PETTY

Fresh Air

Sometimes I feel like I'm actually on the wrong planet, and it's great when I'm in my garden, but the minute I go out the gate I think: 'What the hell am I doing here?' GEORGE

Although we do have control over our actions right at this moment, I think what we are now is a result of our past actions, and what we're going to be is going to be a result of our present actions. So for certain things there's no way out. There's no way I wasn't going to be in The Beatles, even though I didn't know. In retrospect that's what it was, it was a set-up. At the same time, I do have control over my actions. I can do good actions or bad actions. Like I say, I can try being a pop star forever and go on TV and do concerts and be a celebrity. Or I can be a gardener. GEORGE

360   George in the neglected grounds of Friar Park, 1971

I don't go discothequeing and things like that where people hang out with their cameras. So they presumed that I was Howard Hughes. But I wasn't like that at all. I go out a lot of the time, see friends, have dinner, go to parties. I'm even more normal than, you know, normal people.
GEORGE

362   *Above and Right*, George and Peter Sellers, Friar Park, 1974, from George's camera

The seven-headed Dark Horse, Ucchaishravas
Right, George and Olivia, Friar Park, 1977

364   *Page 366–67*, Eric Clapton and George in a garden, 1973, from George's camera

He'd garden at night-time until midnight. He'd be out there squinting because he could see, at midnight, the moonlight and the shadows, and that was his way of not seeing the weeds or imperfections that would plague him during the day, so he could imagine what it would look like when it was done. He missed nearly every dinner because he was in the garden. He would be out there from first thing in the morning to the last thing at night. DHANI HARRISON

It was one of these beautiful spring mornings, I think it was April or something like that, and we were just walking around my garden in the Surrey hills with our guitars. And I don't do that – this is what George brought to the situation. He was just a magical guy and he would show up, get out of the car with his guitar and come in and start playing. You'd have a cup of tea. We walked down in the garden and started playing. The sun was shining, and it was a beautiful morning and he just started to sing, 'Here Comes the Sun', the opening lines, and I just watched this thing come to life. I felt very proud that it was my garden that was inspiring it. ERIC CLAPTON

George's handwritten plant labels
Right, George in the garden, 1973, from George's camera
Pages 370–71, George and Maurice Milbourne, former head gardener, Friar Park, from George's camera

Left, George and Olivia, Tasmania, 1982, from George's camera
Above, George and Hau bush roots, Hawaii
Pages 374–75, Sanskrit mantra, Hawaii, from George's camera   373

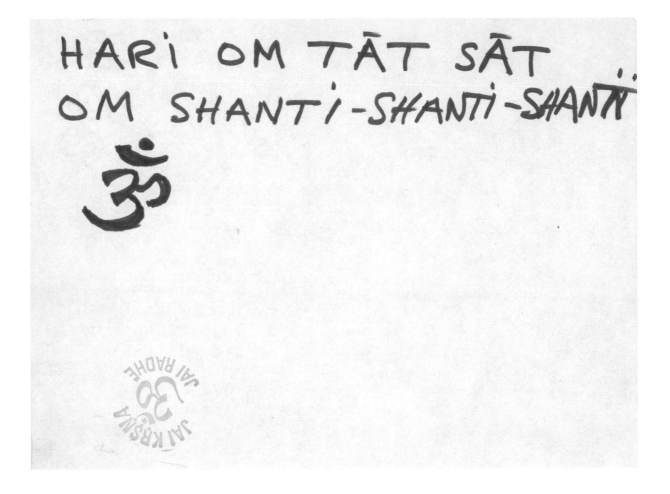

My earliest memory of my dad is probably of him somewhere in a garden covered in dirt, some–where hot, a tropical garden, in jeans, khakis, covered in dirt just continuously planting trees. I think that's what I thought he did for the first seven years of my life. I was completely unaware that he had anything to do with music. I came home one day from school after being chased by kids singing 'Yellow Submarine', and I didn't understand why. It just seemed surreal: why are they singing that song to me? I came home and I freaked out on my dad: 'Why didn't you tell me you were in The Beatles?' And he said, 'Oh, sorry. Probably should have told you that.' DHANI HARRISON

George and Dhani, Hawaii, 1991

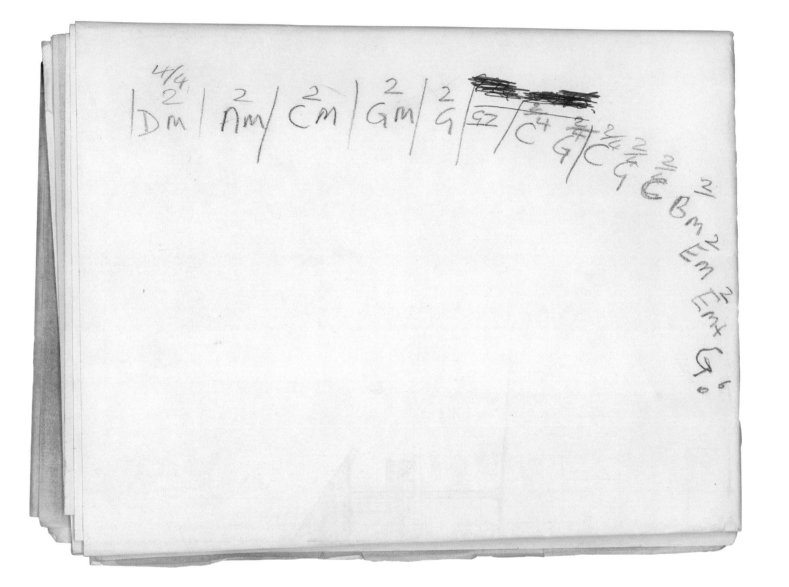

I play a little guitar, write a few tunes, make a few movies, but none of that's really me. The real me is something else. GEORGE

Chords written by George on the back of a map of Maui

Right, George in bamboo, 1999

Olivia, Hawaii, 1987, photograph by George

Right, George during video shoot for 'This is Love', Hawaii, 1987

We went to Fiji – 'take us to the island where there isn't anybody, and then take us in a boat and drop us off on the cove where there isn't anyone' – and then he'd disappear. It's like he's only with me, and then he would go off on his own. But he'd come out dressed in banana leaves or heliconias. For him I think that was just like building a fort out of bracken, exploring nature. His name was George, GEO, 'of the earth', and he really was of the earth. OLIVIA HARRISON

I've just let go of all of that, I don't care, I don't care about records, about films, about being on television or all that stuff because in my eyes that's for people who don't know where they're going. And you know what they say? If you don't know where you're going, any road will take you there. GEORGE

386   *Above and Right*, George, Porto Rafti, Greece, 1979

Nothing I can say about George speaks louder than his music. Knowing how reluctant he was to talk about himself led me to illustrate his years mostly in pictures. His life was fascinating not entirely by chance. He worked hard, was curious and energetic. He plunged into the heart of people, places and things he encountered, the good and bad. He claimed to be a sinner but never a saint.

Life to him was a quest for deeper meaning and everything was important to him but nothing really mattered. His particular way of embracing and dismissing life's joys and disasters was completely disarming. He could let go as easily as I held on. '*Be here now*' was repeated so often we actually did begin to live in the moment.

Time was shortened, stretched and often completely disregarded by his personal clock. At times he moved with the hours and days and then to the rhythm of heavenly bodies in the cosmos. So life was a blink of an eye, but eternal. When he sang, '*Floating down the stream of time, from life to life with me*', he made parting so soon seem like waving goodbye for the afternoon.

George read these words out loud each time we passed the clock tower in the garden. They will always remind me of him and the infinite possibilities of our existence.

Past is gone, thou canst not that recall
Future is not, may not be at all
Present is, improve the flying hour
Present only is within thy power.

OLIVIA HARRISON

I think the two sides of him allowed him to do what he needed to do in this life and have the experiences that he had. When he died there was only one side of him which was the deeply, deeply spiritual person, and he was very set, pointed on one goal, and there was no more mischief or conflict or up and down. There was just one him.   DHANI HARRISON

George on Lake Pichola, Udaipur, India, 1994

Credits and Acknowledgements

Text Credits

All quotes by George Harrison © G.H. Estate Limited

All other quotes © Grove Street Productions except:

p180 David Frost, George Harrison and John Lennon, 'The Frost Programme', © Archbuild Limited

p332 Michael Palin

Picture Credits

Unless listed below all photos are © Harrison Family

Chapter 1, After the Bombs

p14 (detail), p21 photograph from the Stewart Bale Collection, 1941, courtesy National Museums Liverpool;

p17 photograph by Hans Wild, 1941, © Time & Life Pictures/Getty Images;

p18/19 photographer unknown, 1941, © Trinity Mirror/Mirrorpix/Alamy;

p28/29, p30 © Dovedale School, Liverpool;

p31 © Harrisongs Ltd;

p48 © Yoko Ono Lennon;

p52 © Getty Images;

p53 photograph by Nat Farbman © Time & Life Pictures/Getty Images;

p62 © Casbah Coffee Club Ltd;

p63 © Mike McCartney, 1981;

p64 © Michael Ward;

p65 © Getty Images;

p66, p67 photographs by Dick Matthews, 1961, © Apple Corps Ltd;

p69, p74/75 photographs by Peter Kaye, 1962, © Apple Corps Ltd;

p70/71 © Max Scheler / K&K;

p72/73 © Michael Ward;

p76 photograph by Max Scheler © K&K/Redferns/Getty Images;

p77 photograph by David Steen © Camera Press, London;

p79 photograph by Les Chadwick, 1962, © Apple Corps Ltd;

Chapter 2, Mach Schau

p80 (detail), p83 © Gunter Zint/K&K;

p86/87, p88/89 photographer unknown © K&K;

p91 photograph by Astrid Kirchherr, 1961, © K&K;

p96 photograph by Danny Wall, 1962, © Redferns/Getty Images;

p97, p98/99 photographs by Ulf Kruger, 1962, © K&K Ulf Kruger OHG/ Redferns/Getty Images;

p107 photograph by Jurgen Vollmer, 1961, © Redferns/Getty Images;

p109 photograph by Peter Kaye, 1962, © Apple Corps Ltd;

p110, p111 photographs by Dezo Hoffman, 1962, © Apple Corps Ltd;

p112 photograph by Jane Bown © Camera Press, London;

p114 photographer unknown © unknown;

p116, p117, p118, p119 all © Norman Parkinson Ltd, courtesy Norman Parkinson Archive;

p132 photograph by David Hurn, 1964, © David Hurn/Magnum Photos;

p133 photographer unknown, 1963, © BBC Photo Library;

p135 photograph by Philip Jones Griffiths, 1963, © Philip Jones Griffiths/ Magnum Photos;

Chapter 3, A Puff of Madness

p158/159 photograph by Larry Ellis, 1964, © *Daily Express*;

p160/161 photograph by Terence Spencer, 1963, © Apple Corps Ltd;

p163, p165 photographs by Leslie Bryce, 1964, provided by Apple Corps Ltd;

p167 photographs by Bob Flora, 1964, © Bob Flora/UPI/Bettmann/CORBIS;

p177 photograph by Otto Storch, 1965, © unknown;

p178/179 photograph by Mal Evans, 1967, © Apple Corps Ltd;

p181 photographer unknown © ITV/Rex Features;

p183 photograph by Bob Whitaker, 1967, © Camera Press, London;

p184/185 photograph by Mark and Coleen Haywood, 1967, © Redferns/
Getty Images;

p195 photograph by Jan Persson, 1969, © Redferns/Getty Images;

p198/199 © Jill Krementz;

p202 photograph by Ethan Russell, 1969, © Apple Corps Ltd;

p205 © Mal Evans;

Chapter 4, Pilgrimage

p228, p240 © Harrison Family, published by Harrisongs Ltd;

p238/239 all © Roger Siegel. Provided by The Bhaktivedanta Book Trust
International, Inc www.Krishna.com;

p241 © Barry Feinstein, 1970;

p258, p259, p260, p262/263 all © Gary Wright, 1974;

p261 photograph by Olivia Harrison © Harrison Family;

Chapter 5, All Things Must Pass

p264 (detail), p267, p272/273, p274/275, p277, p278/279, p284, p285, p287
all © Barry Feinstein, 1970/1971;

p266 © Harrison Family, published by Harrisongs Ltd;

p270 © unknown;

p271 photograph by Richard DiLello, 1971, © Harrison Family;

p276 © Harrison Family, published by Harrisongs Ltd;

p281 © Harrison Family, published by Harrisongs Ltd;

p289 © Harrison Family, published by Harrisongs Ltd;

p290 photographer unknown, 1971, © unknown;

p291 © Jim Horn, 1971;

p292, p293 photographs by Henry Diltz, 1971,
© Henry Diltz/morrisonhotelgallery.com;

p294 courtesy of Jim Keltner;

p300/301, p303 photographs by Jan Steward, © Umlaut Corporation;

p306/307, p311 photographs by Clive Arrowsmith, 1974, © Umlaut Corporation;

p308/309 photograph by W Roy Hudson, 1973;

p313 photograph by Tom Monaster, © Tom Monaster Photography;

p314/315 © Henry Grossman;

p317 photograph by David Hume Kennerly, 1974, © Getty Images;

Chapter 6, Handled with Care

p321 photograph by Jill Furmanovsky, 1981, © Jill Furmanovsky;

p327 © Harrison Family, published by Umlaut Corporation;

p328/329 photographer unknown, 1981, © unknown;

p331 photograph by Caroline Irwin, 1981, © Umlaut Corporation;

p332 logo courtesy of Handmade Films;

p333 photographer unknown, 1982, © unknown;

p335, p339 photographer unknown © unknown;

p337, p340 © John Townsend/Formula One Pictures;

p345 photograph by Alberto Tolot, 1988, © T. Wilbury Limited;

p347 © www.brianaris.com, 1979;

p349 photograph courtesy of Alan Rogan;

p352/353 photographs by Don Smith, 1988, © T. Wilbury Limited;

p354, p355 © T. Wilbury Limited;

Chapter 7, Fresh Air

p360/361 © Barry Feinstein, 1970;

p364 photograph by Jack Katz, 1974, © Harrison Family;

p365 photograph by Clive Arrowsmith © Harrison Family;

p373 photograph by Brian Roylance © Genesis Publications.

p376, p379, p381, p383, p385, p386, p387, p393 all photographs by
Olivia Harrison © Harrison Family

Acknowledgements

Special thanks from Olivia to:

Mark Holborn for being in tune.

Martin Scorsese, Jeff Rosen, Paul Theroux, Andrew Wylie, Scott Pascucci, Eric Himmel, Margaret Bodde, Leslie Boss, Rachel Cooper, Lisa Frechette, Solveig Karadottir, Mary McCartney, Rachel Wickens.

David Costa at Wherefore Art? for his artistic guidance.

Apple Corps archive department: Aaron Bremner, Dorcas Lynn.

Louise Harrison, Harry and Irene Harrison and Peter and Pauline Harrison, family of Mal Evans, Jim Horn, Jim Keltner, Mike McCartney, Alan Rogan, and Gary Wright for use of their family photographs.

Yoko Ono Lennon for kind permission to reproduce John's letter.

Very special thanks to G. from O. and D. Harrison

Editing of interviews by Oliver Craske
Design by Jesse Holborn / Design Holborn
Project Manager, Richard Radford
Photographic restoration and retouching by Gena Paul Roylance
Picture rights by Amanda Russell and Blair Foster

Library of Congress Cataloging-in-Publication Data

Harrison, Olivia, 1948–
  George Harrison : living in the material world / Olivia Harrison ; edited
by Mark Holborn.
      p. cm.
  ISBN 978-1-4197-0220-4
  1. Harrison, George, 1943-2001—Pictorial works. 2. Rock
musicians—England—Pictorial works. I. Holborn, Mark, 1949– II. Title.
  ML420.H167H37 2011
  782.42166092—dc23
  [B]

                        2011020231

Compilation and Text © 2011, Harrisongs Limited
Foreword © 2011, Martin Scorsese
Introduction © 2011, Paul Theroux and Harrisongs Limited

Printed and bound in the United States of America
10 9 8 7 6 5 4 3 2 1

Abrams books are available at special discounts when purchased in quantity for
premiums and promotions as well as fundraising or educational use. Special editions
can also be created to specification. For details, contact specialsales@abramsbooks.com
or the address below.

3/21
2/28

115 West 18th Street
New York, NY 10011
www.abramsbooks.com